REVIEWS
CREATIO
BOOKS

Second Edition

Edited by Liz Rank Hughes

**First edition edited by Stan Weinberg
with the assistance of Paul Joslin**

**The National Center for Science Education, Inc.
Berkeley, CA**

Library of Congress Catalog Number 92-050337

ISBN 0-939873-52-4

©1984, 1992 The National Center for Science Education
Second edition, published 1992

The reviews of the following books were reprinted with permission:
  Physics of the Future from *Creation/Evolution Newsletter*
  The Origin of Species Revisited from *Free Inquiry* 11(3)
  Of Pandas and People from *Bookwatch Reviews*
  Evolution: A Theory in Crisis from *Zygon* 22(2)
  Darwin on Trial (Bauer's review) from *Journal of Scientific
    Exploration* 6(2)
  Darwin on Trial (Gould's review) from *Scientific American* 267(1)
  The Natural Limits to Biological Change from *Creation/Evolution
    Newsletter*
  The Mystery of Life's Origin from *Creation/Evolution Newsletter*

Published by the National Center for Science Education, Inc.,
P.O. Box 9477, Berkeley, CA 94709.

Printed and bound in the United States.

CONTENTS

PREFACE

In the ten years since the first edition of this book came out (as *Reviews of Thirty-One Creationist Books*), much has changed in the creation/evolution controversy. The teaching of evolution has been firmly supported by the courts, and laws mandating the teaching of creation "science" in public schools have been dismissed as unconstitutional. The vigor with which creation "science" is pressed upon public schools has not decreased, however. (If anything, it is stronger than it has been in decades.) But it is occurring more quietly, more locally. Instead of pushing headline-making legislation, supporters of creation "science" are taking the battle to individual classrooms and school boards across the country.

The books they are using to support their case are a mixed lot. A wide assortment is reviewed in this volume. About half the reviews from the first edition are included here, with only minor revision. Many books reviewed ten years ago are still in print, substantially unchanged, in spite of their numerous deficiencies. Others, though out of print, are still widely available and continue to be cited, and are thus included. And many new books have been published in the last decade. Some are simply old wine in new bottles, but others approach the controversy with more sophistication (real or apparent), and thus warrant longer reviews in this book. A few are critical of both creation "science" and overly broad claims for evolution. They are included since they speak to many of the important issues raised in this controversy, although they are not creationist books in the sense that the majority of books reviewed here are.

As in the first edition, reviewers were given free reign with style and amount of supporting references. This book is not intended as a scholarly treatise, but primarily as a source for those who are faced with these creationist books in their lives as teachers, parents, school board members, and concerned citizens.

Many thanks to Stan Weinberg and Paul Joslin for the concept and execution of the first edition of this book; to all the reviewers, many of whom worked on very short deadlines; and to Genie Scott for guidance and encouragement.

Funding for this edition was provided by The Richard Lounsbery Foundation and the Esther A. and Joseph Klingenstein Fund. Reviewers' professional affiliations are provided for identification; the opinions stated in the reviews are those of the reviewers, and not necessarily those of their institutions or organizations, or of the Richard Lounsbery Foundation, the Klingenstein Fund, or the National Center for Science Education.

Liz Rank Hughes, Editor
November, 1992
Seattle, WA

PREFACE TO THE FIRST EDITION

The reviews in this book were conceived in 1982 during a drive by Iowa creationists to install their books and other materials in the schools of sixty Iowa communities. Some of the targeted school districts turned to two local, cooperating, pro-science groups for evaluations of the books that were being pressed on them. The two groups were the Iowa Committee of Correspondence (CC), and the Iowa Academy of Science Panel on Controversial Issues. (The latter group is now dissolved.) In response to the appeals, six of the reviews included here were welcomed, and they proved useful to school boards, administrators, teachers and librarians. Thereafter, various factors caused the list of books under review to grow. Ten titles comprised the rest of the immediate list that creationists were promoting; when Bert Thompson come from Alabama to conduct a pro-creationist "crusade" in Iowa, his book was added to the list; and so on. In the end the drive was frustrated; not one of the sixty targeted communities actually adopted the creationist materials for its school libraries or classrooms. Indeed, the creationists abandoned their effort after failing to gain a foothold in about twenty-five communities where they had tried.

The reviews in the book differ among themselves. In length they vary from one to six pages. Three reviews are illustrated, the rest are not. Some of the evaluations are cursory, others are quite detailed. A number of reviews are thoroughly documented while others list no references at all. The editors provided minimum guidance while encouraging the authors to express their individual viewpoints. Thus the variability in the book is to a degree intentional. For example, since creationist literature is highly repetitious, it seemed redundant to provide a reference list with every paper.

On the whole the reviews are unfavorable. This is necessarily so since the literature of "scientific creationism," as the book abundantly illustrates, tends to be meretricious pseudoscience. Yet the reviewers took pains to offer kind words whenever this was possible. At least two of the books — Aw, *Chemical Evolution*, and Young, *Christianity and the Age of the Earth* — while criticized, are nevertheless treated with respect because of their honest tone and the substantial amounts of accurate science that they contain.

Besides the named authors, thanks are due to many who contributed to the production of the final work. Paul Joslin generously assisted the principal editor, besides doing some of the editing himself, as noted above. Lee DeMoss is responsible for the cover as well as for the art work inside [the first edition of] the book. Lawrence P. Staunton, Leland Johnson, Harlo Hadow, Donald M. Huffman, Clifford G. McCollum, Donald H. Shepherd, Thomas E. Fenton, Donald L. Biggs, Erik P. Scully, and Robert W. Hanson refereed the papers; most of the referees also contributed manuscripts of their own. Philip Kitcher, Richard Bovbjerg, and Gerald Skoog were valued consultants. The book was put together on a lean budget with substantial volunteer help, as noted here; but the task was eased by a most generous grant from the Iowa Academy of Science. We trust our readers will find that the product is worth the effort. *Stan Weinberg*

FORWARD

In March of 1992, a reporter from a central Illinois newspaper called me about a story she was working on about evolution and creationism in the local schools. She had discovered the good news: no creationism was being taught. The bad news was that no evolution was being taught, either, the teachers just quietly deciding to avoid a "controversial issue." A parent she contacted confided in her that although she was concerned about whether her son would be at a disadvantage when he went to college next year (yes), she "couldn't get into this. I don't want my kids to be picked on for being *devil worshippers*."

Evolution a "controversial issue?" In the 1990s? Wasn't all this settled with the Scopes trial in 1924? Certainly, it must have been settled with the Supreme Court *Edwards v. Aguillard* decision in 1987, striking down a Louisiana law requiring the teaching of creationism whenever evolution was taught. Wasn't it?

No, it was not. And, yes, evolution is a controversial issue in the 1990s, right up there with sex education, AIDS education, and supposedly "Satanic" elementary school reading texts. Evolution is taught less frequently in 1992 than in 1982 because of parental pressure on teachers, occasionally because of official or unofficial policy, and most frequently because teachers anticipate "problems" from the community.

"Scientific" creationism is the latest salvo of antievolutionism to afflict American education. It is a movement of Biblical literalists, overwhelmingly Christian, who feel not only that the world was created in six, twenty-four hour days, a few thousand years ago, but that this view can be supported with *scientific* as well as theological evidence. Because they have an alternate "science," they argue for equal time in the classroom.

"Scientific" creationism was born when a 1962 Supreme Court decision, *Epperson v. Arkansas*, declared that it was unconstitutional to ban the teaching of evolution. Subsequently, antievolutionists tried to ameliorate the teaching of evolution by teaching the Bible along side it; this approach was swiftly struck down by Federal District Courts. Then came the notion that by calling Biblical literalism "science," it could validly have a place in the public schools. Creation "science" was declared religious advocacy in a 1987 Supreme Court decision, *Edwards v. Aguillard*. This has not noticeably slowed the movement down. The Supreme Court only interprets the Constitution; it does not enforce the law. When it comes to the creation/evolution controversy, laws are frequently low on the list of concerns; of greater importance is community sentiment, especially in the small towns and religiously homogeneous communities in which nearly half the American population lives.

The first edition of this book, titled *Reviews of 31 Creationist Books*, was produced by the Iowa Committee of Correspondence to give libraries, teachers, and schools the information they needed to evaluate unfamiliar books which were being thrust upon them by well-meaning citizens. This second edition, renamed *Reviews of Creationist Books*, has been produced for precisely the same reason, only more so: in the 1990s, we face an even more determined scientific creationist movement than faced a decade ago.

This book should be considered a tool for understanding and challenging creationist imperatives. It contains reviews by scientists and teachers of the most frequently-encountered creationist books which are used to challenge evolution and promote "scientific" creationism. When creationists suggest that the textbook, *Of Pandas and People* is a useful supplemental text for the high school biology class, *Reviews* will help to make the argument that this book is poor science. When creationist parents suggest to a teacher (as they will, sooner or later!) that material from one of these books should be incorporated into the curriculum or into the teacher's treatment of evolution, *Reviews* will help to make the argument that our students should be receiving only the *best* science education, not the shoddy science found in the books reviewed. *Reviews* is an excellent source of information on both popular and less well known creationist claims and the arguments against them, whether or not they have yet surfaced in your community. Like *Voices for Evolution*, *Reviews of Creationist Books* is intended to be taken to school board meetings, given to principals, shared with teachers, and in general, used to defend the integrity of science education.

We are pleased to offer this expanded and revised publication. Use it!

Eugenie C. Scott
Executive Director, NCSE

CHEMICAL EVOLUTION

by S.E. Aw
Master Books Division, Creation Life Publishers
San Diego, CA (1982)

Chemical Evolution is unusual among creationist books in that S.E. Aw is inclined to treat his own specialty, biochemistry, in a thorough and scholarly way. The most serious errors in the better parts of the book lie in Aw's failure to understand the significance of data which he usually presents accurately. These misunderstandings afflict both the large scope and the details of his book. The last third of the book deteriorates so badly that it cannot be recommended even to confirmed creationists looking for support from a qualified scientist.

Most of *Chemical Evolution* is devoted to attacking scientific hypotheses concerning the origin of life. What Aw fails to understand is that the current scientific inquiry into the origin of life is largely irrelevant to the theory of evolution. The theory of evolution is about the evolution of life. It is strongly supported by geology, paleontology, and various parts of modern biology. No evolutionist would claim that any sketchy hypothesis about the origin of life is part of, or has the power of, the theory of evolution.

Scientists have produced suggestive experiments that make it easier to imagine that life originated by natural processes. Given that no one makes very strong claims for the resulting hypotheses, Aw's book could be said to document striking progress toward an understanding of the origin of life. However, suppose we accept every detail of Aw's critique of these hypotheses. We could conclude that science does not yet understand how life began, but Aw's conclusion that evolution is "directed" by other than natural processes is unwarranted.

In fact, by accepting Aw's critique we go too far. In addition to being irrelevant to the theory of evolution, Aw's attack on hypotheses concerning the origin of life is seriously flawed. His arguments are largely "God of the gaps" arguments. Of course science doesn't understand everything, but that doesn't make everything it understands wrong. Little more than a century ago science had not recreated a single biochemical reaction, and it was widely held that all of biology was "directed" by a "vital force." But the gaps are constantly filled. (Until recently, "scientific" creationists pointed to the gap in the fossil record between land animals and whales and made "scientific" arguments that "proved" it was impossible for such evolution to have occurred. Coincidentally, at about the time *Chemical Evolution* went to press, transitional whale fossils were found in India.)

Aw begins by trying to demonstrate that the ancient, reducing atmosphere needed for most (but not all) theories of the origin of life could not have lasted long enough for life to appear. By page 13 he concludes: "A period of 2 billion years or so, thought to be available for chemical evolution, has now retracted to less than a billion years. This poses an acute problem as to whether a type of organism such as that found in the Onverwacht chert, could have evolved within the time available." Never mind that he has just finished telling us the Onverwacht Series "were of

1

relatively inconsistent morphology and their biogenic nature is as yet uncertain." In fact, biologists are delighted to see the origins of life pushed back in time, and no evolutionist would suggest that the difference between 1 and 2 billion years is significant. We could even accept Aw's highly questionable suggestion (based on Brinkman) that the earth had an oxidizing atmosphere through "99% of its history." The one remaining percent of its history is still 45 million years, and we have a pretty good idea what could have happened in 45 million years.

Although the formation of organic compounds in the ancient, reducing atmosphere was probably not as efficient as it is in the laboratory, it is possible that lightning alone could discharge enough energy to cover the surface of the earth with a layer of organic compounds 1 meter thick in only 100,000 years. (Ultraviolet light was probably a still more important source of energy.) We have no record of it, but it is certainly conceivable that the formation of more or less living material coincided with the formation of the earth.

To attack the idea that life began by natural processes, Aw needs to do more than show that there are gaps in science. (If there were no gaps, science would stop.) Aw needs to show that life could not have begun naturally. He comes closest to attempting such a proof when he tries to show that an enzyme could not have been assembled from its amino acids by random processes. (Enzymes are proteins which cause specific chemical reactions to occur more rapidly. By and large, enzymes determine what you are.) This is an argument which, if correct, could be directed against the theory of evolution as well as origin-of-life hypotheses.

The chains of amino acids that make up enzymes are complex, but complexity is not a sign of "directed" assembly. Complexity can be found in chaos even more quickly than in order. If the protein structures that are found in living things were the only structures that would serve their functions, if they were even the simplest, Aw would have a point. However, any single, randomly generated protein is likely to be an enzyme that affects the rates of thousands of reactions. There is an old, but serious, piece of advice among organic chemists: "When you can't get the reaction to go, spit in the reaction mixture." Some protein in the spit is likely to be the right enzyme. The evolutionary problem is not to produce an enzyme; it is to eliminate unwanted enzymes and side effects.

Consider the absurd complexity of the blood clotting system. There are dozens of proteins involved, some in more than one way. If exactly those proteins were required, evolution could not explain clotting. However, clotting is a property of any large, randomly produced protein solution. The problem is not to create proteins that clot, but to remove those proteins that clot at the wrong time. That is a chore to which evolution is admirably suited. The clotting system is complex, because it is selected out of chaos by the removal of unwanted proteins. If its creation were directed, the clotting system would be simpler. In the same way, all other functions of living organisms are based on properties which are common among proteins.

Aw's probability arguments are exactly analogous to this: Suppose I tell you Iowa won the basketball game last night. Aw says, "Oh, what was the score?" It was 80 to 76, so Aw says, "The probability of a basketball

2

game ending at 80 to 76 is only one in 10,000. Therefore, Iowa didn't win the game last night. Not only that, basketball doesn't exist." There are many ways to make an enzyme just as there are many ways to beat Purdue. The rules of the game force any particular outcome to be unlikely.

Further into the book I was unpleasantly surprised when Aw dredged up the creationists' old argument about the second law of thermodynamics. The second law states that the amount of order in a closed system cannot increase spontaneously. (A tower of bricks will fall into a pile, but a pile of bricks won't fall into a tower.) Aw states "... some physicists ... are unable to explain to their own satisfaction the apparent contravention of the second law of thermodynamics in living things...." Twenty pages later Aw clearly states that he knows better: "It used to be thought that living things do not obey the second law until it was realized that they are open systems." I don't know who, other than creationists, ever thought living things violate the second law. A living cell no more violates the second law than a General Motors assembly plant does. An assembly plant increases the order in the parts of a car by putting them together. It does so by using energy from the outside in conformity with the second law. A living cell increases its own order by using energy from outside the cell.

Aw then ducks into a description of irreversible thermodynamics "as a branch of classical thermodynamics." Apparently we are to hope, as he must, that irreversible thermodynamics might do for creationism what classical thermodynamics fails to do. His description sounds erudite but only reveals that irreversible thermodynamics is a subject he hasn't studied. It has almost nothing to do with classical thermodynamics. In particular, it does not contain laws that limit the kind of universe we live in. Rather it is a set of phenomenological equations whose parameters may be adjusted to fit any universe.

As the book wears on we find misleading, out-of-context quotes, misrepresentation of the conventional view of evolutionists, and arguments against straw men. By page 165, Aw resorts to red-baiting, strongly suggesting that evolutionists are atheists and often even communists. Such material alone, in what is asserted to be a book of science, makes the book unacceptable for school use.

David Vogel, Ph.D.
Department of Oral Biology
Creighton University School of Dentistry
Omaha, NE 68178

PHYSICS OF THE FUTURE
A Classical Unification of Physics

by Thomas G. Barnes
Creation Life Publishers
El Cajon, CA (1983)

Thomas G. Barnes, D.Sc., professor emeritus of physics from the University of Texas at El Paso, believes that the universe is less than 10,000 years old. The former dean of the Institute for Creation Research (ICR) graduate school uses arguments from decay of the earth's magnetic field and rate of recession of the moon to support his claims. Knowing this should prepare you for *Physics of the Future*. Barnes claims to have laid the groundwork for a revolution in physics. It is, rather, a regression. The foundations of modern physics, in particular relativity and quantum mechanics, are rejected. It is an act of courage — the author attacks these two highly successful theories with the barest of analytical tools.

To Barnes, physics has abandoned "common sense," and emphasizes mathematics at the expense of observation. This remarkable statement is followed by Barnes' own rambling version of armchair science. His goal is to show reasons why quantum mechanics, special and general relativity, wave-particle duality, and atomic and nuclear theory should be rejected, and how phenomena these theories so successfully explain can be accounted for by classical physics. All forces of nature, he claims, can be reduced to two forces: electrical and magnetic. Furthermore, he reinstates the concepts of luminous ether, absolute time, and absolute space. To explain nuclear forces, he develops models for the electron, proton, and neutron that are novel, if not rigorous. Inertial mass is considered an electrical phenomenon, as is gravity.

Of course, this book is worthless as science. It is interesting only for its importance to the creationism controversy. Barnes is cited by creationists as an expert *in physics*. When this "expert" exhibits such hopeless incompetence *in his field of expertise*, and his works are still praised by his creationist colleagues, the low level of their collective proficiency is obvious.

The theories Barnes rejects have useful, well-known applications. I know of no group that objects to modern physics on religious grounds. For these reasons, the public may be more receptive to this book as evidence of incompetence among creationists that they are to arguments against creation "science" biology or supporting evolution.

I can't go into all of Barnes' speculations here, but will only note some of the more outstanding problem.

Barnes discusses relativity from a position of blissful ignorance. First, he holds up the "twin paradox" as a refutation of special relativity. Barnes may find a freshman level lecture on relativity illuminating; the twin paradox is resolved through a straightforward application of relativity theory. The same is true of the "proof" of the existence of absolute space (i.e. rotating reference frames must be rotating with respect to something; obviously, it's absolute space). According to Barnes, physicists who "ride the Einstein bandwagon" refuse to recognize this, or perhaps they delude themselves. To say that distant masses in the universe define a preferred reference frame is an inconsistency, according to Barnes, since he doesn't know the difference between and *absolute* and a *preferred* frame of reference. (Make that a high school lecture on beginning physics.)

Wave-particle duality is similarly rejected. A particle cannot exhibit wave properties, says Barnes, nor can a wave exhibit the attributes of a particle. For example, Barnes would agree that a particle cannot exhibit diffraction or interference. But he doesn't discuss the well-known evidence for diffraction and interference of particles. He must know about electron and neutron diffraction. A university professor of physics must know the results of the double-slit diffraction experiment. A forthright discussion of wave-particle duality must include this evidence, especially a discussion that disputes the theory. Yet, all this is conspicuously absent from Barnes' book.

Barnes does discuss two items of evidence for the quantum of light: the photoelectric effect and Compton scattering. Here again, a rudimentary understanding of these phenomena will be helpful in enjoying the professor's exposition. When light shines on a metal surface, electrons are ejected. This is the photoelectric effect. It has some interesting features; Barnes mentions some of them. First, for a given metal, only light above a certain frequency will cause electrons to be ejected. Second, the maximum energy of the electrons depends on the frequency of the light, but not its intensity. Barnes explains it as "an internal resonance within the atom." Later, he states that the resonance may lie "in the vestibule of the molecule." Details are sketchy, but presumably, incident light of a certain frequency will excite this "internal resonance," and the atom (or molecule, or vestibule) will absorb energy until an electron can be ejected. Strangely enough, energy is released from the atom in quanta proportional to the frequency of the incident light. That's Barnes' theory. What really happens is this: a quantum of light is absorbed by a free electron at the surface of the metal. If the absorbed energy exceeds the surface binding energy of the electron, it is ejected. Since the energy of a photon is proportional to its frequency, only photons above a minimum frequency will cause electrons to be emitted.

Barnes' theory predicts a peak in the energy of the photoelectrons when the incident light is of the resonant frequency. Barnes reproduces an equation which shows that the maximum energy of the photoelectrons increases *linearly* with increasing frequency, with a slope that is *the same for all metals*. He also conveniently forgets to mention that the photocurrent begins almost immediately after light hits the metal, even at extremely low intensities. There's no time for an atom to absorb energy until it can eject an electron. Barnes' theory has no explanation for either of these effects. An expert in physics would know this. No doubt Barnes will continue to search for "the correct interpretation," but the quantum of light explains the photoelectric effect simply and precisely, and unifies it with many other phenomena.

A photon scattered by a free electron will change wavelength. The change in wavelength depends on the scattering angle; it can be calculated by treating the photon and electron as colliding particles and applying conservation of momentum and energy. This is Compton scattering. Once again, quantum theory predicts the effect precisely. Barnes offers no quantitative alternative. Instead, he quotes Ralph Sansbury, who states that the Compton effects is due to "the production of 'oscillations of charge' in the scattering material which in turn produce resonant ejection of a photon and/or the secondary x-ray radiation and recoil of a free electron," and G. Burniston Brown, who says "the change in wavelength of [the waves] is a Doppler effect." This is sheer nonsense. Radiation scattered by reradiation from an oscillating charged particle is of the same wavelength as the incident radiation, in the classical case. The wavelength of Compton scattered radiation at a particular angle exhibits two peaks, one scattered by free electrons in the target at a longer wavelength, and one scattered by bound electrons at the incident wavelength. There is no classical explanation. The calculation from quantum theory is exact.

These are just the beginnings of Barnes' fanciful physics. His atomic model includes big, spongy electrons, tiny protons, and nothing else. A neutron consists of a proton embedded in an electron. In fact, a neutron differs from a hydrogen atom only in the relative orientation of the proton and electron. The author insists these models are "tentative." "It will take years ... to work out the precise relations but it appears that the classical approach can provide the answers."

All this illustrates the differences between Barnes and legitimate scientists. Science searches for unifying principles. Some outstanding examples of such principles are quantum mechanics, relativity, and evolution. Barnes offers his "new theory of electrodynamics," which is really a patchwork of ad hoc hypotheses. His only interest is in explaining the data he knows, and he doesn't know many. Each experimental result is considered individually, and requires a new classical "explanation." This is perfectly consistent with "scientific" creationism, but not science.

Scientists must be willing to subject their theories to tests. Barnes shows no willingness to test his conjectures. He thinks he knows the data, he gives what he thinks is a reasonable explanation, and that's the end of it. It's the data he doesn't know that show him up.

A scientist strives to be quantitative. Barnes makes a few stabs at it, when he knows the right answer. When he doesn't, his results are dismal. In other cases, as in his "explanation" for the Compton effect, he doesn't even try. This is most important. Despite its power as a unifying principle, the theory of evolution by natural selection is not particularly quantitative. The public has difficulty distinguishing between evolution and creation on this basis, especially when religious prejudices are involved. In the quantitative realm of physics the flaws in Barnes' theory, and his competence, take on new clarity. After seeing Barnes' use of the usual creationist tactics in his book, the same foolishness stands out in other creationist writings as never before. This is the only possible reason for reading this otherwise worthless book.

You may wonder about Barnes' motives. He yearns for "the early days of physics, when physics was known as *natural philosophy* [and] common sense was at a premium." A recurring theme in the book is that physicists are indoctrinated "in a philosophical acceptance of 'no need to be concerned with cause and effect relationships'." Barnes echoes the claim of every pseudoscientist that there exists an "elite," which maintains its position by intimidation, indoctrination, and suppression. Furthermore, "it is the author's hope that this book will encourage young independent scientists to take heart, abandon that nonsense, be original and fruitful in science, and enjoy a more wholesome philosophy." He may truly be concerned about "leftist" philosophy in modern physics, but I'm left with the impression that his main objection to modern physics is that he just doesn't understand it.

This review was originally published in *Creation/Evolution Newsletter*, and is reprinted by permission.

Charles A. O'Donnell
M.S. Nuclear Engineering, Electrical Engineering
Manager of Quality Assurance
Roseville, CA

ORIGIN AND DESTINY OF THE EARTH'S MAGNETIC FIELD

by Thomas G. Barnes
Institute for Creation Research
Technical Monograph No. 4
Institute for Creation Research
El Cajon, CA (2nd edition, 1983)

In this book, Barnes claims to show that the Earth can be no older than 10,000 years. His hypothesis is based on the undisputed observation that the strength of the Earth's magnetic dipole field has decreased approximately 6 percent since 1835. Barnes asserts that the field is decreasing because the source of the field is freely decaying currents circulating in the fluid iron-nickel core. He claims that these currents originated by unknown processes when the Earth was created and that the decay of the resulting magnetic field is irreversible and exponential, with a half-life of 1400 years. He calculates that the Earth's magnetic field would have been impossibly large in 8000 B.C. and concludes that the Earth must be less than 10,000 years old.

Barnes disregards most of what is known about the behavior and history of the Earth's magnetic field. For example, Barnes' calculations are based on observatory measurements indicating that the Earth's dipole-field strength has decreased since 1835. These same measurements, however, also show a corresponding increase in the strength of the nondipole field (which constitutes about 15 percent of the total field), so that the total-field energy external to the core has remained about constant — a fact that Barnes ignores. Barnes consistently errs in equating the dipole field, which is only one idealized component of the real field, with the total field and with the total-field energy. In doing so, he neglects all of the higher order harmonics, collectively called the nondipole field, as well as the probability of a toroidal component internal to the core.

Barnes also attempts to discredit paleomagnetic measurements, which have shown not only that the Earth's field has existed for more than 3 billion years but also that the dipole field both fluctuates in strength and irregularly reverses polarity. In attacking paleomagnetism, however, he fails to cite the extensive literature that clearly demonstrates the validity of this widely used geophysical technique. Barnes denies that there is any source of energy within the Earth to sustain dynamo maintenance of the Earth's field; he seemingly is unaware that radioactivity, gravitational energy, tidal friction, and meteoritic impact during the early history of the Earth provide a more than ample supply of energy for a dynamo within the Earth's iron-nickel core.

Barnes frequently misrepresents the work of others that he cites. For example, he attributes his geomagnetic field-decay hypothesis to Sir Horace Lamb, stating that, "In 1883 Sir Horace Lamb proved theoretically that the earth's magnetic field could be due to an original event (creation) from which it has been decaying ever since." Lamb's 1883 and 1884 papers on this subject, however, were concerned with the theoretical behavior of electrical currents (and their associated magnetic fields) in a spherical conductor; Lamb mentioned neither the Earth's field nor creation. Similarly, Barnes claims that Cowling's theorem precludes a dynamo in the Earth's core. Cowling's theorem, however, only restricts the types of fluid motions that are permissible in the Earth's dynamo — a point clearly stated by Cowling but ignored by Barnes.

These are only a few examples of the gross factual errors and distortions that pervade this book. For those interested in learning more about the scientific shortcomings of Barnes' hypothesis, it has been thoroughly refuted in the articles by Stephen Brush (*Journal of Geological Education*, 30:34-58, January 1982) and myself (*Journal of Geological Education*, 31: 124-133, March 1983).

Although the book's cover proclaims that this is a "revised and expanded edition," it is actually little different from Barnes' first (1973) effort. The only revisions include some minor changes in the brief introduction and the addition of two short sections to the end; one in which Barnes claims confirmation of his "theory" and issues a nonsensical challenge to "skeptics," and another in which he unconvincingly replies to some of his critics.

It is a pity that Barnes made no effort to reorganize his prose for this second edition. The main body of the text still consists of four separate articles, three of which were published previously in the *Creation Research Society Quarterly*. The result is that the book is uneven, inconsistent, and highly repetitive. The level of treatment varies from the elementary ("The poles of a magnet are called the north pole and the south pole") to the abstruse ("Expanding the Laplacian of vector A in spherical coordinates..."), so that it is not at all clear to whom the book is directed. The introduction proclaims that the book is "... intended to be useful to the layman as well as the scientist." The layman, however, will find large parts of it confusing and incomprehensible, and will be misled by the myriad of errors in both fact and logic; the knowledgeable scientist will find the book either amusing, outrageous, or both.

In summary, this book is so permeated with scientific errors, omissions, misrepresentations, and distorted logic, and is so poorly organized and written, that I can conceive of no legitimate educational or scientific use to which it could profitably be put.

G. Brent Dalrymple, Ph.D.
U.S. Geological Survey
Menlo Park, CA 94025

THE ORIGIN OF SPECIES REVISITED
The Theories of Evolution and Abrupt Appearance

by Wendell R. Bird
Philosophical Library
New York, NY (1987, 1988, 1989)

A two-volume work by lawyer Wendell R. Bird, titled *The Origin of Species Revisited: The Theories of Evolution and Abrupt Appearance*, appeared in September 1989, following long publication delays. Each of its two volumes runs to about 550 pages; each deals with a different set of topics. Volume I, subtitled "Science," carries most of the text relevant to Bird's theory of abrupt appearances. Volume II deals with philosophy of science and religion, history, education, and constitutional issues.

Seasoned creationist-watchers will find little or nothing new in Bird's work. Instead, they will be inundated with redundancies and quotations. Most of the latter are brief, and nearly all are from the publications of scientists described as not being proponents of "either the theory of abrupt appearance or the theory of creation" (I:1)*. Bird intends no endorsement of either theory by these citations.

This article is is limited to an attempt to analyze certain key problems Bird's theory presents. I shall not cover the arguments for or against naturalistic evolution and for or against recent divine creation (creation "science"). These have been dealt with at great length in several recent books and numerous journal articles (see for instance Strahler 1987).

Bird distinguishes three theories for comparison and analysis (I:1): the theory of evolution (E); the theory of abrupt appearances, or discontinuitist theory (D); and the theory of creation (C). The letters E, D, and C are mine, used hereafter as code symbols of the three theories.

The complete definition of theory D reads as follows: "The theory of abrupt appearances is defined as scientific interpretations of scientific data postulating origin through discontinuous abrupt appearance in complex form" (I:18). You may ask, "What kinds of objects make their alleged 'abrupt appearances'?" Examples: a species or genus of an organism; a continent or ocean; a planet, star, or galaxy; the entire universe. The last six words of Bird's definition are crucial to our analysis, especially "discontinuous" and "in complex form." He leaves two interpretations open to us: (1) no prior existence, that is, appearance *ex nihilo*; (2) prior existence in a noncomplex (simple) state.

Theories E and D are characterized as constituting a "noncreationist" class (I:7). Theory C is described as "a scientific theory of creation" and requires or assumes belief in a creator (I:7). In a footnote Bird uses the expression "either the theory of abrupt appearances or the theory of creation" (I:1). This disclaimer that D is not C and C is not D is important to him. Bird goes to special pains to make clear that D "... does not necessitate reference to a creator or ad hoc explanation based on acts of a creator ..." (I:25).

---

* Shorthand used here for "Volume I, page 1"

The theory of abrupt appearances (D) is vulnerable in four categories of analysis, discussed below.

I. Existential nature of the theory of abrupt appearances: Illusion or reality?

The theory of abrupt appearances, or discontinuities (D), can have either of two existential interpretations: the first, obviously intended by Bird, is that the "abrupt appearance" of a particular entity (thing) is a real phenomenon in nature, existing completely independently of its being known or inferred by humans from historical records as presently available and documented.

I propose as an alternate interpretation that the alleged "abrupt appearance in complex form" is a fiction arising from the intrinsic nature of the historical record, which is simply an incomplete set of observations of what was actually a continuum. Thus prior non-existence is not the reality but only an illusion created by seeming absence in one time period of what humans have observed to be present and documented at a subsequent time. Put another way, the history book as written was complete and accurate, but now many pages are missing.

The distinction between the above two interpretations can be illustrated by a time-lapse camera fixed in place and taking exposures at intervals of, say, one hour. The camera is focused on a patch of clear sky. At the same time, a video camera continuously records the same scene. Now, within a few minutes after a time-lapse exposure has been taken, a tiny speck of cloud appears in the frame of blue sky. It grows steadily in size and continuously changes in outline, and at the end of the hour has become a dense, lofty cumulonimbus cloud. Later, the two records are viewed by several persons, none of whom saw the original event. As the time-lapse film runs, the initially blank frame abruptly presents the huge cloud. "Look at that!" a viewer exclaims, "The huge cloud appeared instantly from nowhere!" "Just wait!" cautions the video camera operator, starting to play the video tape. "You'll see the cloud continuously grow and evolve from a mere speck." Only an irrational person would claim that every sudden appearance of an object leads to the logical conclusion that the object never preexisted.

The logical defect in Bird's theory of abrupt appearances is that while observation can safely lead to the conclusion that an object exists in a particular state when first observed, the implication that it did not exist that way in the prior time cannot be inferred. It is not possible to demonstrate inductively the empirical existence of nothing. Moreover, the phrase "existence of nothing" (existence of nonexistence) is a self-contradiction.

The problem does not lie in establishing the existence of what has appeared, for that can be observed by evolutionists, discontinuitists, and creationists alike. The uniqueness of Bird's theory (D) vis-à-vis the evolution theory (E) lies in that which precedes the appearance, that is, in the antecedent condition or state prior to the discontinuity. The condition or state that follows the discontinuity is common to both theories and is not in dispute.

We search Bird's volumes in vain for an unequivocal description of the antecedent condition or state. In effect, then, there is no meaningful statement of Bird's theory. We shall need to construct that statement ourselves as best we can in a logical fashion.

II. Consequences of a purely empirical theory of abrupt appearances

How abrupt is "abrupt"? One of Bird's formal definitions of his theory reads as follows (I:25): "First, 'abrupt appearance' is properly defined as scientific data and scientific interpretations that indicate discontinuous abrupt appearances but not supernatural causes." In another context, specifically that of the seemingly abrupt appearance of taxa (orders, classes, phyla) as described by evolutionary scientists, Bird allows for two different meanings of "abrupt" (I:52). For geologists, he notes, "abrupt" may refer to deposition of enclosing strata occurring over spans of tens of thousands of years. Obviously, then, the geologists' meaning requires a continuum rather than a discontinuity, and is thus ruled out as a postulate of theory D.

Bird makes clear that theory D implies that abrupt appearance is instantaneous appearance, and we will adopt that meaning. His work contains no further refinement of the definition of "abrupt" or "instantaneous" that is quantitative in the mathematical sense. So we are left with accepted dictionary definitions, and from them must make a more precise formulation, using principles of mathematical logic. We refer first to *Webster's Ninth New Collegiate Dictionary* (1985).

"Abrupt" (adj) is from the latin *abruptus*, "to break off." The idea of termination is clear, and this is unfortunate because we wish to imply beginning rather than ending. The various definitions allow some choice of context but little precision.

The Webster definitions of discontinuity and discontinuous are mathematically precise and can be used effectively. For the former term, a noun, we read "2: gap (a break in continuity) ... 3a: the property of being not mathematically continuous. b: an instance of being not mathematically continuous; esp: a value of an independent variable at which a function is not continuous." This information is what we need to treat Bird's theory as if it were genuinely scientific in content.

Bird's theory D tells us that matter appears instantaneously in a complex state, either *ex nihilo* or from a primitive noncomplex prior state. It is important at this point to establish rather precisely the meaning we shall assign to the term matter and its intended relationship to energy. Two frames of reference need to be included: (1) classical (Newtonian) mechanics; (2) relativistic mechanics. Classical mechanics applies quite satisfactorily to the range of distances and velocities encountered in the physics and chemistry of our planet and solar system. In the symbolism of dimensional analysis used in classical mechanics, the components of mechanics are manipulated as products of time, length, and mass. All three dimensions appear in the definitions of energy, momentum, and related terms, such as force, stress, work, and power. In relativistic mechanics, where rest mass varies with velocity, mass and energy become interchangeable. Physicist Kenneth R. Atkins describes this relationship as follows: "Mass and energy can be considered to be different manifestations of the same physical quantity. A quantity of energy E ... can always be considered to have a mass E/c^2. Conversely, the mass m of a material object can be considered to be the equivalent to an amount of energy equal to mc²" (Atkins et al. 1978:107).

The above definition of matter is relevant in our analysis of the conflicting theories E and D, because they are applied on dimensional scales ranging from the subatomic, atomic, microscopic, and small scales of planetary physical/chemical processes to the vast scale of the entire universe. Thermodynamics and entropy change are correspondingly applied over this same enormous scale range.

We refer next to the principles of the calculus of classes that define explicitly the nature of operations and relations of classes. We will treat the competing theories – evolution (E) and abrupt appearances (D) – as statements about real classes of matter. Members within a particular class are characterized as having or lacking specified states or configurations of matter in a common reference framework of time and space. (Examples of classes: all galaxies, all volcanoes, all individuals of one species or of one genus.) Thus, the class "galaxies" contains the set, or collection, of all individual galaxies.

We use the following definitions and relations relating to classes. A class is a group of individuals each having certain common properties by reason of which they are said to be members of the class. Classes are designated by letters a, b, c, etc. For our purposes we will be discussing real classes – those having members in an empirical sense. A null class (or zero class), logically possible, is without any members in the empirical sense; it is designated by zero. The universe of discourse (domain of discourse) consists of classes whose relationships we have chosen to discuss.

For both of our competing theories, one class (a) precedes in time (t) another class (b). Only theory D requires that the following initial postulate be applied throughout all of the history of our universe: At some point in time, t_i, the class a is instantaneously replaced by class b. Under theory D, there are innumerable t_i points at which a prior class, a, has been followed by a distinctly different class, b. (Note that for the *ex nihilo* assumption, class a is a null class.) The number of such discontinuities is without limit. Under theory E (evolution), there can be introduced be only a single t_i, which would be the cosmic singularity described below, but no pre-evolutionary state or history is required to be specified. All of evolution following the singularity is a continuum in which one class evolves into another class without a mathematically instantaneous discontinuity. The elapsed time between transition from one class to the next in unbroken succession can be relatively slow or relatively rapid, but is always finite. Figure 1 suggests this finite period of transition in contrast to the instantaneous case.

A brief statement of a widely held modern theory of origin of the universe is useful at this point. Cosmologists who support the Big Bang theory define a point called the cosmic singularity, when all matter was contained in a single point (Kaufmann 1985:522). The density of that matter was infinite, and space and time did not exist as separate entities. Moreover, space and time did not obey the laws of physics. Cosmologist Joseph Silk clearly identifies the cosmic singularity with "the initial instant of time" in reference to the Big Bang theory (1980:22,61-62). For the case

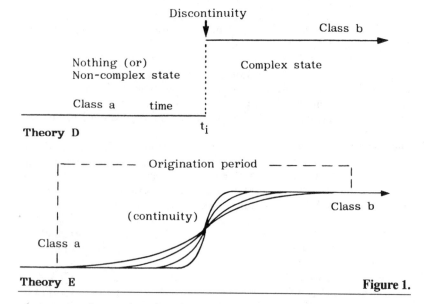

Figure 1.

of an open universe, there is only one singularity. That "singularity" implies "zero-time" (t_o) is self-evident by the designation of the times of later events with respect to that instant. This definition of "singularity" is important in enabling us to arrive at a precise description of Bird's theory of abrupt appearances.

Whether or not a store of matter existed prior to the singularity is a question capable only of being speculated upon in any scientific sense. If the answer is "No," the singularity will correspond with our t_i, separating the null class from all real classes; if "Yes," no t_i is required and no null class need be included the the universe of discourse. Neither alternative affects the theory of evolution (E), broadly defined as an unbroken, lawful continuum of changing configurations of matter, because its initial point would in either case first be defined at Planck time, occurring approximately 10^{-34} second after the singularity. After Planck time a radiation-dominated universe was in place with a set of laws to govern all relationships and changes (Kaufmann 1985:524). The theory of evolution does not depend on any specified condition antecedent to Planck time.

In Volume II, Bird throws some possible light on the nature of an abrupt appearance. He presents us with a most remarkable concept, namely, "a natural law of the abrupt appearances" that applies only in those "singular events" or "initial singularities" (II:95). He describes his law thus:

> Second, although a natural law of abrupt appearance would involve a natural law different from those visibly operating today, the same is necessarily true of each phase of evolution. That is, if natural laws govern the key points of evolution, they must be natural laws different from those operating today in the cases of cosmic evolution (the origin of matter and energy contrary to the second law of thermodynamics and the big bang through or preceded by different natural laws), of biochemical evolution (the

origin of life contrary to the laws of biogenesis and statistical probability), and of biological macroevolution (the origin of higher categories of organisms contrary to the capacity of natural selection and other mechanisms and contrary to the laws of genetics and statistical probabilities). (II:96)

The sad thing about all this is that Bird fails to state his "natural law of abrupt appearances." He does not state it because it cannot exist; because it is not logically possible. The natural laws scientists have formulated since the dawn of modern science deal with the functional relations (relationships) observed to exist between two or more different classes of information within the universe of spacetime and matter. In its functional statement, one variable changes in reponse to changes in related variables; i.e., $y = f(x, z, ...)$. Examples: law of gravitation (relation between force and mass, between force and distance); laws of motion (relations between mass and velocity or acceleration); First Law of Thermodynamics (energy in one form transformed into energy in another form); Second Law of Thermodynamics (relation of entropy (unavailable form of energy) to heat added and to temperature).

Now, an abrupt appearance gives rise to a single real class (b), containing the complete entity that instantaneously appears. If the antecedent class (a) is a null class there is no real antecedent condition to which b can be related. If class a is real, but noncomplex, of a totally different kind than the complex class b, there can be no application of any law (relationship) to the instantaneous change from a to b, because Bird's law lies only in the time domain of class a, whereas laws of science lie only in the time domain of class b. In any case, the real class b cannot be functionally related to any prior state of matter, nor can it be functionally related to t_i, because the duration of that time is an infinitesimal approaching zero. Moreover, Bird states that an abrupt appearance has no dependence at all on any particular time frame, i.e. upon relative or real time (I:27). Because no natural law can be formulated without expression of a functional relationship involving time, and Bird's "law" can have no such dependent relationship on time, his "law" is not possible of existence. Small wonder, then, that he does not attempt to state it.

Confirmation that Bird accepts the requirement of instantaneous appearance is found in his later statements in Volume II, introducing his "law of abrupt appearances." Here he states that "natural law of abrupt appearances would involve initial singularities" (II:96). Why is it necessary under the theory of abrupt appearances that "abrupt" be defined as "instantaneous" in the sense that the duration of the event be an infinitesimal element of time approaching zero as a limit? The reason is that, if any finite period of time were required for the complete appearance of an object, the origination (construction process) of the object would be spread over that time span through a range of degrees of completeness that would run from zero to unity. Consider, for example, the "abrupt" appearance of the first member of the extinct species *Archaeopteryx lithographica* (the earliest known fossil bird). Let us postulate that a formative period of, say, one year qualifies as being "abrupt." Early in the year this creature's appearance began with the tip of a single claw, followed by several claws and a foot, and within a week or so, by a whole leg. Near the close of the year the head and beak were added, and finally on the last day, the feathers. Obviously, for most of the entire period this "thing" would be an incomplete, non-functional organism. That first leg would have decomposed long before it could receive blood circulation. An all-powerful Creator could easily avoid such difficulties by supernatural means, but he is unavailable as an agent under the restrictions imposed on the theory.

Next, we must consider a corollary under theory D: no change of state or configuration of matter is possible after each t_i. In other words, total stasis of class b follows any t_i. Change is logically excluded on grounds that change is exclusively reserved for the alternative theory of evolution (E), and theories E and D are mutually exclusive, being subject to the law of the excluded middle (II:169). Therefore, change has no role in nature under D.

There appears now another possible corollary: if, for D, no change of state or configuration of matter is possible after an abrupt appearance, then that configuration endures forever into time. If so, and if each abrupt appearance is the formation of something from nothing (*ex nihilo*), then each abrupt appearance adds to the universal store of matter, in violation of the first law of thermodynamics. If no change is possible after the abrupt appearance, no energy can be transformed from an available form into an unavailable form, so that no increase in system entropy is possible. Thus the second law of thermodynamics is inapplicable. It follows then that no change of entropy is possible except by repeated abrupt appearances of new matter, and these would always decrease total system entropy. Creationists, those who espouse the theory of creation (C), depend on a universal and non-reversible increase in entropy as part of their religious dogma, so they would not be happy with the theory of abrupt appearances that invokes *ex nihilo* origination.

Another interesting logical product of the theory of abrupt appearances (D) is that the successor principle, essential to the theory of evolution (E), as well as to all empirical science through modern mathematics and mathematical logic (Russell 1920:20-28), has no place or meaning within D. This conclusion is clearly implied by Bird, who states that (D) "... does not require any particular time frame for the universe or life" (I:27). We can conclude from his statement that D allows for any time-order of specific appearance events, which could range from purely random occurrences to a single instant of appearance of everything in the universe.

In the random case, *Homo sapiens* could have appeared before the first atoms of hydrogen and helium in the primeval universe. That thought alone should point to the absurdity of freeing D from any time frame. The alternate possibility of simultaneous appearance of everything in the universe would have the advantage of possibly (but not necessarily) providing *H. sapiens* with a sustaining environment. Simultaneous creation is nicely exemplified in Philip Gosse's Omphalos, but that version requires a Creator and is off-limits to us here. (It's very difficult to keep the Creator out of the theory of abrupt appearances, but a discontinuitist mustn't yield to that temptation, else all be lost.)

What we have uncovered is a preposterous, monstrous concoction, offered by Bird as a serious empirical theory of the universe we observe today. Every logical deduction his theory spawns leads us farther away from what empirical science finds a lawful and reasonable (if incomplete) model of the evolution of the universe through a continuum of physical, chemical, and biological changes, constantly reforming and restructuring its initial store of matter. The total requirement of numbers of abrupt appearences during the history of the universe is staggering. Each galaxy and each star in the universe requires its own separate abrupt appearance. Using data from Kaufmann (1985:473,554), we can calculate that there are at least one million (10^6) galaxies with 100 billion (10^{11}) stars in a typical galaxy. Multiplying, we get a total of 10^{17} stars in the universe, every one requiring an abrupt appearance. Turning to all biotic taxa, from species up through phyla, we can use data of Raup and Stanley (1971:11) assembled from various sources. Estimates of the number of fossil species since life began range from 50 million to 4 billion. Without even adding the progressively smaller numbers of each higher taxon, that's a tremendous number of abrupt appearances of new species! If you wish to claim that God created all these galaxies, stars, and species, all well and good, because he can do that sort of thing with one hand tied behind his back. But the discontinuitists ask us to believe they just happened abruptly with no creative or causative agent whatsoever. Are you prepared to swallow that?

There is, of course, a path of partial redemption for the discontinuitists, but it lies in a painful and messy compromise with the theory of evolution. To deny that evolutionary change is occuring in the universe today is unthinkable. Change of configurations and states of matter is an inescapable characteristic of the real world. Open systems and subsystems of mass and energy are seen everywhere in continual flux. A hurricane can be observed to form, intensify, weaken, and dissolve. We can document the demise of a comet as it vaporizes and disperses in close proximity to the sun. All stars are observed to fit into a life history of initial formation from gas clouds, followed by orderly changes in temperature and density, often leading to an explosive end in a supernova that returns much of its substance to the gaseous state and diffused dust. A supernova is nothing if not change, and even though its optical presentation may come to us a million years after the event, reveals a mode of change that, though relatively sudden and rapid in relation to the star's total life span, is continuous in time; its antecedent and consequent states are well established.

The classic example of compromise already made by the discontinuitists is their recognition of microevolution in living organisms. Genetic change is obvious through its expression in the genetically stable phenotypic varieties produced by artificial selection in the breeding of domesticated plants and animals. "Yes," the discontinuitist says, "we do slip in a little bit of evolution, but it merely follows upon an abrupt appearance (of the species) that is incapable of explanation by the evolutionary mechanism."

III. Fitness of the Theory

We turn now to evaluate the fitness of Bird's theory of abrupt appearances. Is it deserving of recognition as an empirical scientific statement? Is it worthy of being designated a scientific theory or hypothesis? Is it testable and thereby falsifiable? If so, does it rate high in fecundity?

Bird asserts that the theory of abrupt appearance (D) meets most of the various definitions of science (as he has previously summarized them) as well as does the theory of evolution (E). Important is his assertion that "It involves empirical data and scientific interpretation" (II:81). There is no question that theory D as stated deals with empirical data. That which appears abruptly is clearly identical in description with the same observable entities with which the theory of evolution deals. When Bird includes "scientific interpretation," we must blow the whistle and flash the red lights.

First, the meaning of "interpretation" must be clarified. From *Webster's Ninth New Collegiate Dictionary* we find the word to mean "to give the reason for or cause" and "to show the logical development or relationships of." Both are acceptable explicit definitions.

For a statement to qualify as being scientific does not require interpretation or explanation. Bird (II:25) aptly cites Quinn (1984) in making the distinction between existence and explanation, where "explanation" includes the application of natural laws. It can be genuinely scientific simply to demonstrate the existence of a phenomenon, which at the time cannot be explained in terms of causes and natural laws. Laudan (1984) is quoted by Bird as supporting this position. Bird adds Quinn's further claim that some scientific phenomena can have no explanation in terms of laws. Accepting these points, we can grant that the theory of abrupt appearances, as stated, can be accepted as a scientific statement. But is it also explanatory? Definitely not.

Bird makes a desperate attempt to introduce explanation into his theory: "Discontinuitist scientists suggest that abrupt appearances and sytematic gaps are explained most naturally and logically by discontinuity or unrelatedness of the natural groups of plants and animals" (I:50). That's merely a repetition of the statement of the theory or hypothesis itself; i.e. it's tautological. He offers no explanation at all; no process is referred to and no description given of how a species is assembled or from what materials.

A scientific theory (hypothesis) that describes a complex state or system of matter must be judged seriously deficient and perhaps impotent if it lacks a lawful explanation in terms of both the origin and the processes of change that are involved in its operation. The purported scientific theory of abrupt appearances is simply devoid of these requisites; it is instead entirely an existential assertion.

As to testability and falsifiability, Bird claims that the theory of abrupt appearances qualifies for both (II:81). For testability, Bird gives a long list of supposedly testable claims (II:104-106). On examination, these are claims of what is observed after the instant of appearance. They are not tests deduced from the theory, which is the postulate of the singularity itself and the nonexistence or noncomplexity that preceded it. The existence of the referent entities and their properties after their appearance is not an essential or unique part of the theory.

Is there a testable deduction (prediction) arising from the essence of the theory of abruptness, that relates to what existed prior to the instant of singularity? What is there to predict or deduce? We might try to phrase a possible test in these words: If the theory is correct, no prior existence of the entity or phenomenon will be found. This ploy fails, because as we stated earlier, the existence of nothing cannot be demonstrated by observation within range of the finite. Searching and not finding would need to be carried to the limit of infinity of space and time before it became a valid test. The theory itself contains no causal explanation, so there are no causes to test. The theory simply cannot be tested or falsified.

How does the theory of abrupt appearances stand up in application of the three positive characteristics of successful science, as described by science philosopher Philip Kitcher (1982:48)? They are as follows: (1) Independent testability, "... achieved when it is possible to test auxiliary hypotheses independently of the particular cases for which they are introduced." Obviously, from what has been concluded above, such testing is not possible. (2) Unification, "... the result of applying a small family of problem-solving strategies to a broad class of cases." For this theory, there is only one problem-solving strategy: the singularity of an abrupt appearance. It can perhaps be broadened to provide that everything in the universe has originated and continues to originate from nothing in a nonstop singularity, sweeping through time and always locked precisely on the present. The theory of abrupt appearances can score A + on this one, just as does Gosse's Omphalos version of instant creation by a supernatural creator, complete with evidence of a prior state that never existed. Both are sheathed in impenetrable armor covered by a leakproof teflon epidermis. (3) Fecundity, that "grows out of incompleteness when a theory opens up new and profitable lines of investigations." The theory of abrupt appearances flunks that one dismally; it opens up nothing new whatsoever.

IV. The Probability Argument

The argument from probability, often closely linked with the argument from design, is considered by creationists to be one of their strongest arguments, even though they often suffer self-inflicted wounds when they try to use it. Bird is no exception in this respect, as we shall see, running into logical difficulties as he applies the argument to his theory of abrupt appearances, or discontinuities (D) vis-à-vis the theory of evolution (E).

Bird's claim is basically that the vast information content of complex molecules and of complex structures of any kind in the physical/chemical and biological makeup of the universe provides affirmative evidence favoring D, while at the same time providing strong evidence against E (I:76). The referent structure might be, for example, a single-celled organism, the neuronal system of the human brain, the DNA content of a chromosome, or the entire universe itself. Information content as a measure of complexity is a comparatively new quantitative concept accompanying the age of computers. It refers to the number of stored information units (bytes) needed in correct sequence to describe something fully. One byte stores the memory of one character, either a letter or a number. Repetitions (redundancies) of the same byte sequence generally do not increase information content. For a complex naturally-occuring object (i.e. not an artifact) such as the human eye or brain, for which the ordered informational sequence runs into the billions of bytes, it is most tempting to conclude that because the probability is so extremely small, an external agent must be responsible and that it is a Supernatural Intelligence, otherwise known as a Creator, alias God.

The discontinuitists, under their alleged strictly empirical theory (D), claim that the extremely small probability of an abrupt appearance by chance alone is strong evidence in favor of their theory. At the same time, however, they claim that no supernatural intelligence or creator is required or even admissible, leaving the discontinuitists without any causative explanation whatsoever. Randomness or nonrandomness is always descriptive of some real or hypothetical process in action. Discontinuitists simply deny the existence of process. Process, which must by definition involve change, requires time to proceed, whereas the discontinuity infinitesimal of an abrupt appearance approaches zero. Thus, the discontinuitists leave themselves in a position of being unable to apply either of the two logically opposed alternatives: (a) random or (b) nonrandom. Probability estimates are thus not logically connected in any way with their so-called "theory," and by the same token cannot strengthen or weaken their theory. For the same reason, neither can these probability estimates be used to compare the strengths of the theory of abrupt appearances (D) and the theory of evolution (E).

In glaring contrast is the other pair of theories in competition: naturalistic evolution (E) versus supernatural creation (C). For both of these, the question of randomness versus nonrandomness is a legitimate consideration, because both include process (cause) in the explanation of the phenomenon that is observed. For causation by a supernatural Creator claimed to be omnipotent and omniscient, total nonrandomness can be assumed, unless the Creator did a little coin-tossing to resolve difficult choices. In evolution, whether physical or biological, both modes are used. The nonrandom mode is seen in fundamental, lawful determinstic explanation, but with a substantial element of randomness superimposed as an error function.

The Inevitable Connection

Now comes the awful disclosure. Bird and others who attempt to sell the strict discontinuitist position must feel at least a vague, disturbing awareness that their assertions of evidence favoring their theory are invalid. Perhaps that is why in Chapter 2, on biological theory of abrupt appearances, starting on page 80, the word creation begins to appear in quotations stressing the extremely low probabilty of an abrupt appearance.

The establishment of a logical connection between the theories of creation (C) and abrupt appearances (D) is made in Chapter 11, where Bird presents the view "acknowledged by many evolutionist scientists and philosophers" that "the sole alternative scientific explanations of the origin of the universe, life, and plants and animals are the theories of abrupt appearance or creation and the theory of evolution" (II:166). Using our letter code for these three theories this statement reads: "Either D or C vs. E." The two pairs of alternatives present here can be separated into D vs. E and C vs. E. Bird correctly describes these two pairs as "logical sole alternatives, under the law of the excluded middle" (II:169). He rejects the contention of numerous evolutionists that C vs. E is the only choice, preferring instead the alternative D vs. E, because (D) "is based on affirmative lines of scientific evidence" (II:171). Expression of his preference notwithstanding, Bird has perhaps inadvertently made a logical connection between C and D, which is that D is included within C. What D lacks that C possesses is the alleged causative agent of a supernatural creator. All of Bird's lengthy arguments for abrupt appearance (D) apply equally well or badly to creation (C). So, in effect, he has promoted creation (C) with the same best efforts he has made on behalf of the touted "nonreligious" (secular) theory of abrupt appearances (D). We then can infer the possibility that his theory of abrupt appearance is contrived for expediency, namely the necessity of keeping religion out of the legal argument for teaching "creation" science in the science classroom. This contrivance amounts to a denial of a supernatural creator.

Attorney Wendell R. Bird, J.D., is engaged in private practice as head of a law firm in Atlanta, Georgia. A graduate of the Yale Law School, he published in the Yale Law Journal a paper arguing "... that exclusive public school instruction in the general theory of evolution ... abridges free exercise of religion" (1978:518). His preferred solution: to "neutralize" that situation by teaching both evolution and "scientific creationism" (p. 570). The paper received widespread attention. Bird then drafted a model school-board resolution designed to allow teaching of "scientific creationism" as an alternative explanation to the standard science model of biological evolution. It was published by the Institute for Creation Research (Bird 1979). Bird served as general legal counsel to the ICR from 1980-82. In 1987, as special counsel for the State of Louisiana, he argued before the U.S. Supreme Court for *Edwards v. Aguillard*, a major test of the 1981 Louisiana law authorizing teaching of "creation science" in schools of that state.

References Cited

Atkins, Kenneth R., John R. Holum, and Arthur N. Strahler 1978. **Essentials of Physical Science.** New York: John Wiley & Sons.

Bird, Wendell R. 1978. "Freedom of Religion and Science Instruction in Public Schools." **Yale Law Journal** 87(3):515-70.

_____ 1979. Resolution for Balanced Presentation of Evolution and Scientific Creationism. **ICR Impact** No. 71.

Cohen, Morris R. and Ernest Nagel 1934. **An Introduction to Logic and Scientific Method.** New York: Harcourt, Brace, & Co.

Kaufmann, William J. 1985. **Universe.** New York: W. H. Freeman & Co.

Kitcher, Philip 1982. **Abusing Science: The Case Against Creationism.** Cambridge, MA: The MIT Press.

Russell, Bertrand 1920. **Introduction to Mathematical Philosophy.** New York: Simon and Schuster.

Silk, Joseph 1980. **The Big Bang: The Creation and Evolution of the Universe.** San Francisco: W. H. Freeman & Co.

Strahler, Arthur N. 1987. **Science and Earth History: The Evolution/Creation Controversy.** Buffalo, NY: Prometheus Books.

This review was originally published in *Free Inquiry* 11(3) in 1991, and is reprinted by permission.

Arthur N. Strahler
Retired Geologist, Columbia University
Fellow, Geological Society of America

ORIGINS: TWO MODELS

by Richard B. Bliss
Creation-Life Publishers
San Diego, CA (1976)

This is an attractively designed, two-color, paperback textbook designated for use in the secondary grades eight through twelve. The book is simply written and is adequately illustrated by charts, diagrams, drawings, and photos. It was written while the author was science supervisor for the Racine, Wisconsin school system and was test-taught in a comparative study conducted within that system. On the basis of this rather questionable study, Bliss asserts that students learn evolution better when it is taught along with creationism in a two-model mode rather than when evolution is taught by itself.

Bliss submitted his study to the University of Sarasota as a doctoral dissertation. According to David McCalley (1982), the instrumental design used in the research was faulty, and in his interpretation of the data Bliss contradicts himself.

The book consists of an introduction and two chapters, the first chapter devoted to the "evolution model," the second to the "creation model." The introduction explains that these two "scientific models" of "first origins" are based on scientific data, while ultimate causes and meanings involve religious feelings. The two models are divided into "submodels" — thus evolution may be "atheistic," "theistic," or "deistic," while creation is characterized only as "creative design." There is no explanation of what is meant by "origins," or what is "scientific" about a "scientific model," or how the submodels of evolution can still be scientific while defined in religious terms, or what is meant by "creative design," or whether the "creation model" is scientific, religious, both, or neither. Thus the book begins with the never-justified assumption that there are two and only two "models" (theories?) of "origins" which are vaguely scientific but also have some religious content. Certainly the book begins with a confusing conceptual hodge-podge.

Each chapter begins by setting up behavioral objectives. Chapter One then defines evolution as an idea that explains how life developed on Planet Earth; it started as simple organisms and then evolved into complex forms. (Biologists would consider this a very inadequate definition of evolution.)

The text now plunges into the evolutionary topics of diversity, isolation, recombination, natural selection, and adaptive radiation. Each is named but is not described or explained with any degree of adequacy, and the various topics are not tied together into a coherent account of the theory of evolution. All evidence for evolution is said to be indirect. The heterotroph hypothesis is described better than earlier topics. Three brief paragraphs take the course of evolution from unicells to birds.

The geological column is discussed with emphasis on index fossils. The method of dating strata in the column is stated in this grossly incorrect manner: "An index fossil that is supposed to be relatively simple in structure, such as a sponge, would be considered very old, and thus the strata in which it is found would be considered very old also." Of course rock strata are dated absolutely by radiometric and other methods; fossils are used for relative dating.

Geochronology, human evolution, and homology are mentioned, and relevant specimens are named and illustrated. But there is no serious attempt to explain any of these areas. It is impossible to see how a student could gain any adequate notion of what evolution is about from this fragmented and inadequate chapter.

The second chapter opens by stating that the "creation model" was "...developed scientifically by trained scientists that interpret present scientific data about life as the result of original design." Beyond repetition of the term "scientific," it is not explained what is scientific about the "creation model," about creationist interpretation of data, or about the creationist assumption of original design. Separately created basic kinds are assumed, and it is stated categorically that changes in basic kinds are never seen and there is no fossil evidence for such changes.

The flood hypothesis is explained in some depth (no pun intended). The deposition of fossils in existing strata is explained as due to settling during the flood according to relative density and ecological niche — an inference that is rejected by sedimentologists and hydraulic scientists as utterly ridiculous and totally unsupported by any credible evidence.

A long list of assertions purports to be evidence for creation: there is genetic variation only within "kinds," there are no "transitional forms," there are systematic gaps in the fossil record, no organisms ever change into another "kind." These assertions, even if valid, would be evidence against evolution, not for creation. Bliss goes on the unstated assumption that creation can be validated by discrediting evolution — a rationale that is acceptable neither to science nor to logic.

The creationists' standard — and absurd — arguments from thermo-dynamics and probability are set forth, as are the thoroughly discredited arguments based on purported secular decay of the Earth's magnetic field and on purported systematic errors in radiometric dating. As science all this is pretty shoddy stuff.

The text concluded by telling the reader to choose between the two models, since, "You have now heard both models in their general terms." Finally there is a "two-model" bibliography that lists precisely seven evolutionary and seven creationist titles.

No reader would find in this book any basis for making the reasoned choice between two "models" that the author calls for. The information on evolution is inadequate, incomplete, largely erroneous, and unintegrated — a major value of evolution theory is that it integrates biological knowledge. The information bearing on creationism, as science, is absurd.

The book's assumption that its two "models" are equivalent and alternative scientific theories is unsupported and unacceptable. The text improperly confuses scientific and religious concepts. It fails to define science as a discipline concerned only with the natural world and not with the supernatural — as leaving religious ideas and questions to religion and theology. It fails to recognize that science deals only with defined, limited, testable problems in the natural world. Thus "origins" are too vague to be a scientific problem. On the other hand, the origin of species is an acceptable scientific problem that is addressed by evolution theory.

Thus the book fails to teach science in any meaningful way. Most fundamentally, it befuddles the basic distinction — enunciated publicly, explicitly, and even forcefully by Federal Judge William Overton in Arkansas — between evolution as an authentic scientific theory and creation as a religious doctrine masquerading as science. Its numerous and glaring deficiencies make *Origins: Two Models* totally unacceptable for use in any school that proposes to teach twentieth-century science.

Reference

McCally, David, "The Two-Model Approach: A Critique." Paper read at National Association of Biology Teachers Convention, Las Vegas NV, October, 1982, and submitted to **American Biology Teacher**.

Stan Weinberg
Biology teacher and writer
Ottumwa, IA 52501

ORIGIN OF LIFE
Evolution: Creation
by Richard B. Bliss and Gary E. Parker
Creation-Life Publishers
San Diego, CA (1979)

In this little paperback module, Bliss and Parker use what they call a two-model approach, contrasting assumptions and interpretations while encouraging the student to decide which model (evolution or creation) fits the data better. The authors specifically concentrate on chemical evolution to the level of the cell, breaking down the model of pre-cellular evolution into five stages: (1) the early atmosphere (reducing); (2) abiotic synthesis of micromolecules; (3) abiotic synthesis of macromolecules from micromolecules; (4) formation of protocells from the macromolecules; and (5) evolution of phototrophic cells and alteration of the earth's early reducing atmosphere into an oxidizing one. They then look at each of these stages, providing what they consider to be holes in the data, flaws in logical interpretation and extrapolation, and problems with the model (as they have presented it). The major problems they present are: not enough time for chance events to have led to synthesis of cells (or macro-molecules, for that matter); increased order of macro-molecules over their precursors, defying the second law of thermodynamics; the complexity of macromolecules and cells being of a nature that requires the existence of a creator. In the final pages of the book one is led subtly to the conclusion that the creation model is the model best supported by the data that they present.

In my opinion, the most important aspect of this book is its contention that one can deduce the preexistence of a creator from the type of complexity of the product created. This is important because creation requires a creator, and almost all scientists believe that the scientific method is not suitable for proving the existence of God, of testing the hypothesis that God exists. If deducing the designer from the design is logically sound, then examination of current knowledge of abiotic synthesis might not only reveal problems with an evolutionary model, but also be used to prove the existence of a creator to bring about the alternative: Divine Creation.

Bliss and Parker's logic can be seen clearly from this quotation:

> How can we gather scientific data in favor of a creation model? The most natural and reasonable approach is to determine how an object created by man could be identified apart from an object produced by natural processes. Consider a television set, a landscape painting, and an automobile as examples. We know that these objects could not make themselves, no matter what amount of time was involved. Scientists can likewise look for evidence of creation in the kind of design found in living things. (p. 2)

They apply this logic to molecules important to living things, concluding that these molecules are of a degree and type of complexity that precludes their synthesis abiotically through natural processes, and thus requires — and proves — the existence of a Creator.

Archaeologists and anthropologists do deduce the presence of primitive man from the presence of artifacts in geological strata, and thus use the "deducing the designer from the design" method of logic used by Bliss and Parker. That method works scientifically, though, because we can objectively study how people create now, and see if things suspected of being created by primitive humans carry these same "tooling marks." An anthropologist examining a sharp-edged rock suspected of being used as a knife, for instance, can examine the sharp edge for evidence of fracturing caused by blows from other rocks or compression applied near the edge. Microscopic examination of edges produced by various techniques reveals fracture patterns which are specific to a particular tooling technique and are different from "natural" weathering processes. The anthropologist then tools the same type of rock in a way he suspects primitive man did and microscopically compares the edge he created with that on the suspected artifact. If the patterns match, and differ from those produced by other techniques or by natural processes, the anthropologist can conclude that the evidence supports the hypothesis that the rock was tooled by primitive people using techniques that can be replicated in the laboratory. The case becomes stronger if bones of animals associated with the artifact reveal the presence of marks made by the stone knife and if the type of rock contained in the artifact does not occur in the immediate vicinity of the artifact. Other artifacts from the same area make the case even stronger, and so on. Anthropologists can verify the creation of human-made objects by humans because we can study how humans create and then seek objective signs that those creative techniques were used. We are not left saying only, "this is too complex to have happened naturally, so it must have been made by a person"; we can say exactly how and why it is too complex.

Obviously we cannot do the same for creative acts of the sort that might have led to complex macromolecules. If there were a Creator, he left no "tooling marks" on the molecules which have been distinguished from those left by natural processes. More importantly, we cannot observe the Creator at work in pre-living times or even place Him in a laboratory and have Him demonstrate His creating technique so that we can see what "tooling marks" to seek, or how "tooling marks," if they exist on natural molecules, differ from those produced by natural processes. While deducing the presence of designers from the designed artifact leads to testable hypotheses when dealing with human artifacts, then, the situation is not analogous when applied to cells and macromolecules which Bliss and Parker believe are Divine Artifacts. Thus they argue from false analogy, the falseness of which might have eluded them, and would surely elude high school readers. Divine Creation *is not* a testable hypothesis and is outside the realm of science; this book brings us no closer to making it testable.

Since a major argument of this book is an argument by false analogy, I cannot recommend the book for use in science classrooms. There are other less substantial reasons for this recommendation as well.

This book does not demonstrate the way that practitioners of science proceed to do science. Since the Divine Creation hypothesis is untestable, those students of the origin of life who were not satisfied with evidence for the existence of a primordial atmosphere of ammonia and methane did not turn to creation as *the* alternative, but instead sought a different primordial atmosphere. Amino acids have been formed in rich abundance from experimental atmospheres containing cyanide and water, substances found in the gases escaping from volcanos. Presumably conditions inside the core of the earth have been less altered by the aging of the earth than have conditions on its surface, and thus more accurately reflect the condition of the primordial earth. These gases are thus thought to have been produced by volcanos in early times as well. We now have two different sets of gases whose alteration by energy sources of the primordial earth might have led to small molecules which could be synthesized into macromolecules. Both have yielded the building blocks of macromolecules under laboratory conditions. Other scientists now are seeking additional support for these models by examining the composition of the earliest of the earth's rocks and by other techniques.

Perhaps evidence will build which will lead to acceptance of one or the other of these hypotheses. Perhaps new hypothetical atmospheres will be proposed and exposed to scientific scrutiny, and both current hypotheses will be rejected. That is the way science works. It is not forced to accept an untestable "because God made it that way" hypothesis by default, when experimental results or observations from the outside world call a favored hypothesis into question. It instead turns to new testable hypotheses.

Experiments with gas combinations found in volcanos, alluded to in the preceding paragraph, are not mentioned in Bliss and Parker's book. Indeed, there are no journal articles cited in their bibliography which are more recent than 1970 and none from reputable scientific journals more recent than 1969. The most recent book cited under "Evolution books" is 1974. Much has happened since 1974 which is pertinent to the development of pre-cellular evolutionary theory. The microfossils obtained by Barghoorn, Schopf, and others (said to be indistinguishable from laboratory protocells) are now included in General Biology texts as evidence for the existence of protocells before cells evolved. Many laboratory experiments have shown that warming of mixtures of amino acids under several sets of conditions hypothesized for the early earth yield "thermal proteins," which have enzymatic activity, aggregate into protocells, have electrical activity like nerve or muscle cells, and have a primitive ability to reproduce. Protocells are able to make, simultaneously, other small compounds such as small proteins and DNA, thus suggesting the origin of a genetic code. Amino acids order themselves in thermal proteins, indicating that genes did not need to precede proteins. This material is present in current General Biology texts for college classes, and even in up-to-date high school texts, but none of it is included in Bliss and Parker's book. Their book is thus out of date.

In summary, then, I find Bliss and Parker's *Origin of Life/Evolution: Creation* to be out of date, inaccurate in depicting the way scientific knowledge grows, and significantly based on argument by false analogy. I see nothing to recommend its use in public school science classes.

Harlo Hadow
Professor of Biology, Coe College
Cedar Rapids, IA 52402

FOSSILS: KEY TO THE PRESENT

by Richard B. Bliss, Gary E. Parker, and Duane T. Gish
Creation-Life Publishers
San Diego, CA (1980)

This nicely designed, easily read paperback is part of a series of modular, two-model textbooks prepared by Institute for Creation Research staff members for secondary school use. The two-color illustrations, mostly drawings, are attractive. Numerous questions are dispersed through the book, and a two-model bibliography is included.

The text begins by categorizing fossils as the only evidence we have that bears on life in the past, and as helpful in choosing between evolution and creation models. (It is not clear at this point what the models are supposed to explain.) There are brief, clear, simple accounts of some of the methods by which fossils are formed. However, geologists would take exception to the statement that "most scientists agree that flooding provides the best way to start forming fossils." The only geologists likely to agree to this bizarre statement are the few creationist partisans of Noah's geological role.

Twelve major geological systems are described. They are said to be identified by means of index fossils, and are described as "often, but not always ... found in a certain vertical order" called the geological column. In keeping with creationist young-earth presuppositions, no dates or time designations (eras, periods, epochs) are given for the systems in the column. The text says, "Dinosaurs are found in only three systems. These systems are lumped together as the Mesozoic or reptile group" (not Mesozoic *Era*). Similarly, the Paleozoic is called the "trilobite group," not Paleozoic Era.

One of two models, evolutionary-gradualism or creation-catastrophe, can enable us to interpret correctly the incomplete fossil evidence. We can then choose between the models on the basis of which best fits the data. The reasoning here seems circular in that we are asked a priori to choose a model to interpret the fossil evidence, and then to use the evidence to confirm or reject our choice. This rationale is not accepted by evolutionary biologists and geologists, beginning with Darwin. To them, fossils are valuable in elucidating the course of evolution, but they do not provide the major evidence upon which rests acceptance of the occurrence of evolution.

Chapter Two proceeds to carry out a program of checking the two models against the fossil evidence. The method used is to compare actual fossils with fossils whose occurrence would be predicted by each model. A problem here is that prediction is useful in discriminating between two alternative scientific hypothesis, theories, or models only when it is exclusive — that is, when one alternative supports the prediction while the other does not. So the creationist prediction of systematic gaps in the fossil record has no value in validating the creationist model, since evolution theory makes precisely the same prediction.

In any event, various groups of fossil organisms — invertebrates, plants, fish, amphibia, reptiles, dinosaurs, flying reptiles, birds, mammals — are described. In each group, text and illustrations stress the sudden appearance of the group in the geological column and the absence of ancestors, transitional forms, or links to the past. Among vertebrates, classical transitional forms such as crossopterygians, *Ichthyostega*, *Seymouria*, *Archeopteryx*, and therapsids are discussed at some length. In each instance the absence of certain homologies and similarities is cited to refute the notion (not the certainty) that the transitional forms indicate evolutionary relationships. The text continually emphasizes the sudden appearance of each major kind early in the Cambrian, but overlooks two glaring omissions: flowering plants and vertebrates do not appear then. Were there several creations rather than one? The book does not speak to this crucial point.

The central Chapter 2 of *Fossils* very aptly illustrates some standard features of creationist dialectic. One gets the strong impression of an adversarial situation, with the authors stressing selected arguments that support a preconceived belief rather than withholding judgment until all relevant evidence has been judiciously evaluated. The authors urge readers to "search and compare all of the data," yet the book does not do this. It stresses what is missing from the fossil record rather than the enormous amount of material that is there. Fossils do *not* provide the best supportive evidence for evolution; the fields of biochemical genetics, comparative anatomy, comparative biochemistry, embryology, and biogeography provide much stronger evidence. Another point that this book fails to make is how closely other stronger lines of evidence correlate with the fossil evidence.

Many points in Chapter 2 are supported by references to evolutionist authors. Yet the references tend to be out of date, out of context, or misinterpreted. Thus a quotation from a 1958 paper by Axelrod stresses the absence of Precambrian fossils; more recent reports by Barghoorn, Schopf, Glaessner, and others, of extensive Precambrian fossils finds are ignored. Gould and Eldredge's concept of punctuated equilibrium does not include Goldschmidt's notion of "hopeful monsters," as the book incorrectly states.

The last chapter gives brief evolutionist and creationist scenarios of biosphere history based on the fossil evidence. The evolutionist summary gives a reasonable account of the course of evolution (the fact of evolution) without going into the underlying mechanism (the theory of evolution). The creationist summary stresses the argument from design — that a complex structure such as the eye must have been created by design and could not have evolved by natural processes. Some of the evidence from Chapter 2 that contradicts evolution is repeated, and a little new and scientifically unsound evidence of this nature is supplied — the non-existent human footprints in dinosaur beds at Glen Rose, Texas, and some bizarre "flood geology." Concerning the last, the text says in a majestic understatement: "However, much work needs to be done to refine the flood model."

The special pleading in *Fossils* is so glaring that the book does not qualify as a science textbook but as creationist propaganda. It is in fact a tract carrying the message of Genesis in the trappings of science. The reviewer believes that an overt study of Genesis would be an asset to any curriculum. But this book is neither science nor religion nor Bible study. It does not belong in any American public school science classroom.

Stan Weinberg
Biology teacher and writer
Ottumwa, IA 52501

DINOSAUR ABC's

by Richard B. Bliss
Creation-Life Publishers
El Cajon, CA (1986)

DINOSAURS: THOSE TERRIBLE LIZARDS

by Duane T. Gish
Creation-Life Publishers
San Diego, CA (1977)

The books listed above are the only two publications on dinosaurs that I've ever encountered that I can imagine my friends' kids *not* wanting to read. The publishers are quite obviously working hard at pushing the "party lines" and not at delighting kids with information about these universally fascinating creatures.

Dinosaur ABC's is billed as an activity book; it has only nine activities. Four of these nine are connect-the-number drawings, but you are encouraged to "put dino in the ark." Not too great for a 26 letter alphabet! Presented only in black and white, with drawings over-drawn to darken originally faint lines, it appears amateurish and visually unappealing. Biblical citations "proving" the global flood sit cheek by jowl with the possibility of *Elasmosaurus* still living in Loch Ness.

Very little information is given about each dinosaur and some questions seem inappropriate: "If you would have met him [*Tyrannosaurus rex*], would you have laughed?" One healthy suggestion ending the text reads: "There may be dinosaurs that still have not been discovered. Perhaps that discovery will be made by you!" That discovery will only be made in a better book!

Gish's book is slicker, but that does not keep it from proceeding from a basic misunderstanding of what science is all about. It is apparent throughout the text, but begins with the almost unbelievable assertion that creationists *believe* thus-and-so, while evolutionists *believe* ... believe – eek! The scientific method is based on observation and the laws of logic, not belief, in the religious sense.

Several themes thread their way through some otherwise valid discussions about different dinosaur types. These are 1) the lack of "in between" forms proves special creation of each individual type of dinosaur; 2) a global flood (brought on by evil in the world) was responsible for dinosaur extinction; and 3) humans and dinosaurs existed contemporaneously (citing the Glen Rose footprints).

The lay-out of this book is both professional and pleasant to the eye. For a few pages at a time there are lengthy and accurate descriptions of a variety of dinosaurs, but these are always followed by a zinger (such as the lack of known transitional forms "proving" that each kind of dinosaur was created separately).

Two of the more fanciful ideas put forth are that man's sin was responsible for there being meat-eating dinosaurs (which, along with thorns and thistles, are asserted to have only appeared after the fall of man), and a lengthy treatment of the possibility of dinosaurs having been dragons. The discussion of dragons tops the list of "things hard to swallow"; it is based on a mechanism by which the bombardier beetle is able to produce hot, bad-smelling gases from its tail tubes. It is suggested that in "strange, hollow bony structures on the top of their head" chemicals such as those found in the beetle might have produced dragons' fabled smoke and fire.

Besides the not-so-great science found in these two books, what I also, as a Christian, find disturbing is the implication that to *be* Christian the Bible must be interpreted literally. Why keep pushing Leviathan and Behemoth as dinosaurs rather than as characters in some moral tale? At a youthful age when life should be a series of open doors, I fear these books close as many doors as they open. Children *will* encounter material on dinosaurs presented from the evolutionist-scientific point of view. What unnecessary confusion will this engender? What pain and disillusionment will arise? Less, if they avoid these two books.

Marcia Clarke
Catholic high school science teacher
San Francisco, CA

APE-MAN: FACT OR FALLACY?

by M. Bowden
Sovereign Publications
Bromley, Kent (2nd edition, 1981)

Ape-Man: Fact or Fallacy? is written to cast doubt on the evolutionary interpretation of the human fossil record. The author, M. Bowden, uses two approaches: 1) questioning the fossil evidence, and 2) questioning the honesty of human paleontologists.

Questions of Evidence

Bowden barely describes or illustrates the fossils for the reader. He does not give an adequate reference, such as Oakley (6), where the reader might obtain further information. These unfortunate omissions greatly reduce the value of the book. Nevertheless, Bowden claims that "the layman's judgment can be as valid as that of the expert" in this "representation of *all* the relevant evidence" (p. 1) — comparable to believing that *any* car owner can explain the internal combustion engine.

Bowden states that "Neanderthal man was a degenerate form of existing *Homo sapiens*, suffering from malnutrition and rickets, possibly living promiscuously" (p. 173). This unwarranted assertion ignores the standard paper about Neanderthal by C.L. Brace (1), and remains dismissive in view of the renewed Neanderthal debate (8).

Bowden claims that *Australopithecus* "did not walk upright" (p. 176). He disputes D.C. Johanson and M. Taieb's (4) description of the fossil knee joint discovered in the Hadar region of Ethiopia. Bowden insists, "I could find no evidence in print which proves that his knee joint exhibited bipedalism" (p. 220). Yet the paper by Johanson and Taieb lists well-known biomechanical research showing that the fossil knee matches a modern knee (3,5). The author's error of fact illustrates his tendency to ignore or distort any evidence that doesn't support his viewpoint.

Questions of Honesty

Bowden believes that human paleontologists conspire to conceal the "truth of Creationism." He shows no comprehension of the self-correcting nature of scientific work, which regularly causes scientists to expose the errors of other scientists. An outstanding example of this procedure is the famous Piltdown hoax. Bowden cites the affair to draw suspicion towards human paleontologists. He might as well claim that modern medicine is suspect because physicians once prescribed "bleeding by leeches" to cure illness. In fact, the Piltdown hoax was exposed by paleontologists, showing that conspiracy and error in science cannot be concealed forever.

Bowden makes other false charges. On page 244 he accuses scientists of plotting with journalists for harsh treatment of dissidents; on the next page he accuses paleontologists of using "evidence which has been wilfully misconstrued." He accuses Eugene Dubois of withholding information on the "Java man" skulls (pp. 141-2), and charges Marcellin Boule with being "unconvinced that *Sinanthropus* was other than a monkey" (p. 105).

However, a scholarly review (2) of the work of these authors demonstrates the falsity of the charges. Bowden's persistent attack upon Fr. Pierre Tielhard de Chardin constitutes almost 40% of the book (pp. 3-55, 90-137)! Personal attacks and vendettas are not the material of scientific discussion.

This book is typical of the creationist brand of science. It offers no new facts, only disputes the work of others, attacks scientists personally, and supports the irrational view that conspiracies are everywhere in science. The book concludes with familiar apologetics and the contrived dualism (7) of modern creationism. Unlike scientists, the creationists not only answer all present-day questions, but they already know the answers to all future questions.

In grossly misrepresenting the nature of scientific discussion, Bowden's book does a disservice to good science education. It does not deserve a place in any modern science classroom, where coming to understand the nature of the scientific enterprise is far more important than absorbing any particular subject content.

References

1. Brace, C. L. 1964. "The fate of the 'Classic' Neanderthals: a consideration of hominid catastrophism." **Current Anthropology** 5:3-43.

2. ____ 1982. Text of the Debate: "Creation vs. Evolution." Hill Auditorium, University of Michigan, Ann Arbor. March 17, 1982.

3. Heiple, K.G., and C. O. Lovejoy 1971. "The distal femoral anatomy of **Australopithecus**." **American Journal of Physical Anthropology** 35:75-84.

4. Johanson, D. C., and M. Taieb 1976. "Plio-pleistocene hominid discoveries in Hadar, Ethiopia." **Nature** 260:293-297.

5. Kern, H.M., and W.L. Straus 1949. "The femur of **Plesianthropus transvaalensis**." **American Journal of Physical Anthropology** 7: 53-77.

6. Oakley, K. P., B. G. Campbell, and T. I. Molleson, eds. 1977. **Catalogue of Fossil Hominids**, 2nd ed., 3 volumes. Trustees of the British Museum (Natural History), London.

7. Overton, W. R. 1982. "Creationism in schools: the decision in McLean versus the Arkansas Board of Education." **Science** 215:934-943.

8. Stringer, C. B. and P. Andrews 1988. "Genetic and fossil evidence for the origin of modern humans." **Science** 239:1263-1268.

John W. Sheets
Professor of Anthropology and Museum Director
Central Missouri State University
Warrensburg, MO 64093

THE RISE OF THE EVOLUTION FRAUD

by M. Bowden
with an introduction by Henry M. Morris
Creation-Life Publishers
San Diego, CA (1982)

The main point of this book seems to be that the theory of evolution by natural selection resulted from a conspiracy by devious, mean-spirited men whose intent was to bring down Christian religion. Rather than a discussion of evolution, the book is an *ad hominem* attack on character. The book begins by setting up a straw man to shoot at. According to Bowden:

> It is commonly thought that Charles Darwin was responsible for conceiving the basic idea of "Evolution." Those who study the matter further usually agree that Darwin first had doubts about the "fixity of species" as a result of examining the variety of finches on the Galapagos Islands. It is then thought that it was this basic idea which he later developed and expounded in his book *The Origin of Species*, first published in 1859. This idea has been so well publicized over a considerable period of time that it is now the most popular interpretation of these events. However, like many other popular and highly-publicized notions, it is quite false.

Bowden is quite right; the notion is false, or at least misleading. After I read that statement, I looked in the indexes of 22 different college-level introductory biology texts and found only one that did not have an entry for Lamarck or Lamarckism. Even moderately well-informed nonscientists should know that Darwin certainly was not the first to have had evolutionary ideas. In addition, the theory of natural selection emerged slowly over the years during and after the voyage of the *Beagle*, rather than by the flash of inspiration that the passage implies. Finally, it was David Lack's careful study that was mainly responsible for indicating the importance of "Darwin's finches" in evolutionary biology. It is unclear to me how these "facts" detract from Darwin's genius.

In his introduction Bowden also tells the reader that he relied heavily upon a biography of Darwin by Gertrude Himmelfarb, published in 1959 and now, lamentably, out of print. It is, however, still in university libraries, and it turns out that Dr. Himmelfarb is equally uncomfortable with the theory of natural selection, and can hardly be classified as an unbiased source of information. Furthermore, the inadequacy of her scholarship is thoroughly demonstrated in a review of her book by Anthony West (1). I suggest that the interested reader peruse his examples of Himmelfarb's slanted presentation before attaching too much reliability to this source, or before expending too much effort in trying to locate a copy.

Much of the first part of Bowden's book is an attempt to discredit Darwin's intellect and to make him look like the tool of Lyell and Huxley in their supposed efforts to subvert Christianity. In reality Darwin did spend time worrying about the implications of his theory for religion, and it was for this reason, in part, that he delayed nearly 20 years from the time he wrote his first outline of the theory until the publication of *The Origin of Species* (2).

There can be no doubt that Darwin and his colleagues were human. Darwin was interested in the fame that his work would bring him, and for that reason he was distraught when Alfred Russell Wallace sent him a copy of a manuscript outlining his own theory. But a human interest in recognition is quite a different matter from intellectual dishonesty and willful perversion of scientific accuracy, despite Bowden's strenuous efforts to translate one trait into the other.

The book is filled with innuendos and suggestions that are later referred to as established facts. One example will serve to make the point. On page 158 the author discusses the age of comets. He asserts, without reference, that Oort developed a theory involving a reservoir in the universe of comets that stars occasionally trap into orbits. He then asserts that there is not the slightest evidence in favor of this theory, and he cites a religious publication to support the assertion. Still later he refers to this discussion as having established that the universe is young. In this sense the book is great propaganda, especially if it were to be presented to a reader who was inclined to attach truth to everything that appears in print. In short, despite extensive footnotes, the scholarship falls short.

The real reason for writing the book finally appears in a discussion of the evils that evolution has supposedly thrust upon society. The author argues that evolutionary theory is anti-Christian — a charge that millions of devout Christians indignantly reject (3). Bowden is afraid that evolutionary theory can somehow destroy belief in God, and he fears this because *"Once God has been eliminated, then any basis of absolute moral standards is destroyed, and all behavior becomes 'relative'."* [emphasis his] I have seldom seen such an explicit statement concerning the motivation of the creationists.

Toward the end of the book there are some brief summaries of the "evidences" against evolution and the "evidences" for creationism, all of which are hopelessly amateurish and erroneous. New to me was a statement that the speed of light has been decaying since the beginning of time, and therefore all radiometric dating techniques are incorrect and the universe turns out to have been formed around 4004 B.C. The source of this information is, of course, a creationist publication.

In summary, this is a rather crudely done religious tract, and it should be viewed as such. The view of history represented by the author is patently insupportable on objective grounds. The only reason even to be concerned with it is that a novice might be misled into thinking that it represents the "facts" about the development of evolutionary theory, when in fact it is outright propaganda. The book's intent is well summarized by a statement made by Anthony West in his review of Gertrude Himmelfarb's biography:

> The truth is that [it] represents an advanced case of Darwinitis, a complaint that afflicts those ... with strong attachments to pre-scientific culture, who find in the theory of evolution a disturbing and mysterious challenge to their values. It is in some obscure way

helpful to anyone who is menaced with loss of status by the theory to denigrate and diminish the man who formulated it.

To that I can only add that the people who developed and are developing the theory of natural selection were and are probing for correct understanding of scientific laws governing the universe. To suggest, as this book does, that they are conspirators in a Satanic plot could not be farther from the truth. Because of both the malice of its tone and the inaccuracy of its content, the book is entirely unsuitable for use in schools.

References

1. Anthony West, "Book review." **New Yorker**, 35(34):188-201. Oct. 10, 1959.

2. "Belief in God defended in Darwin letter." **New York Times**, December 27, 1981.

3. See, for example, "Scholar opposes 'biblical biology'." **National Catholic Reporter**, March 13, 1981; "Cardinal urges accord of science and religion," **New York Times**, September 29, 1981; "Evolution and creationism." Resolution adopted by the 194th General Assembly, the United Presbyterian Church in the USA, June 28, 1982; Resolution adopted by the 67th General Convention of the Episcopal Church, New Orleans, September 14, 1982.

Richard J. Hoffmann
Department of Zoology and Genetics
Iowa State University
Ames, IA 50011

OF PANDAS AND PEOPLE
The Central Question of Biological Origins

Percival Davis and Dean H. Kenyon
Haughton Publishing Company
Dallas, TX (1989)

Gross Misrepresentation

Of Pandas and People is a wholesale distortion of modern biology. It is straight fundamentalist creationism, but this may not be apparent to many readers because the philosophy is couched in a user-friendly voice, with plenty of slick graphics and nice photographs. The text seems sweetly reasonable, but as one reads farther and deeper, the tone becomes angrier and the distortions of science more pervasive.

This book purports to present for teachers "reliable information on plausible alternatives to evolution to balance their curriculum." What it presents instead is the same old dichotomy of evolution vs. sudden creation that allows no accommodation for intermediate views, for religious scientists or laymen who think that it is possible to approach the ways of God through science, or for scientists who carry out science without a preconceived idea of "intelligent design." The theme of "intelligent design" consists mostly of denying any possibility of evolution, and explaining all the evidence adduced for it as "specially created." Thus, homology cannot result from descent, biochemical similarity must be functional in some way because it is not inherited, and the fossil record is a grand illusion.

Particularly illuminating in this regard is the authors' discussion of punctuated equilibrium as a manifestation of "intelligent design." So species don't change gradually in many or most cases through their brief durations in the fossil record. So they are quickly replaced by very similar (daughter) species, which in turn are replaced through time. Evolutionists recognize this pattern (not mechanism, contrary to the authors) as the groundplan of phylogenetic divergence, regardless of how little or how much change occurs in a single species. Not so with these proponents of "intelligent design." They would have you believe that a Creator plucked up each individual species when its time on Earth was over, and replaced it with a similar, apparently as well adapted, but *not descendant* species.

How could this claim possibly be scientific? How can we investigate it? The authors admit that this is a difficult matter. A lot remains to be done, they conclude, by "design proponents." They say, "... scenarios (about the past) ... win our allegiance by being reasonable in light of the total evidence, not because they are proven. Without observation or testing, as could be done for a theory of planetary motion, there is no 'proof' or 'disproof'." This is a complete distortion. All scientific theories strive to be reasonable in light of all the evidence. Observation and testing are constantly being carried out on the evidence from the fossil record. And *no* theories in science are *ever* "proven."

The fallacies in this catalog of errors are as predictable and shopworn as a Henny Youngman monologue. The text suggests that life appeared at the beginning of the Cambrian, when in fact it is only the hard shells of metazoans that are first found with any abundance during the Cambrian. These particular phyla appear in the record through the whole extent of the Cambrian, probably due more to geochemical than biological processes; and moreover, the first life is nearly 3 billion years more ancient, though the authors neglect to mention this or separate the Cambrian explosion from the origin of life. Gaps in the fossil record are magnified and worried over, and Darwin's "gravest objection to my theory" is once again twisted to mean the absence of biological evidence, instead of the incompleteness of the geological record, which is what Darwin meant. *Archaeopteryx* is hopelessly misinterpreted; the authors have neglected to study the copious work on the origin of birds that has made the last two decades the most exciting for the solution to this question. Several hundred shared derived evolutionary features show that birds are descended from small carnivorous dinosaurs, yet this book tells students that the putative ancestor was a "thecodont," a term that is not even used any more by vertebrate paleontologists. Active scientists in this field no longer consider that fishes gave rise to amphibians, which gave rise to reptiles, which gave rise to mammals. It is manifestly clear, instead, that the first tetrapod emerged from lobe-finned marine forms, that both the true amphibians and the first amniotes diversified from the former, and that amniotes quickly split into lineages leading to the mammals (synapsids) and the true reptiles (including birds). However, the past two decades of research are completely omitted from this text.

Equally shameful is the authors' treatment of homology. They pretend that the Tasmanian wolf, a marsupial, would be placed with the placental wolf if evolutionists weren't so hung up on the single character of their reproductive mode by which marsupials and placentals are traditionally separated. This is a complete falsehood, as anyone with access to the evidence knows. It is not a matter of a single reproductive character, but dozens of characters in the skull, teeth, post-cranial bones (including the marsupial pelvic bones), soft anatomy, and biochemistry, to say nothing of their respective fossil records, that separate the two mammals. About the closest similarity they have going for them is that they are both called "wolf" in English. The same criticism can be applied *seriatim* to the authors' mystifying discussion of the red and giant "pandas."

Finally, there is a warped chapter on biochemistry taken wholesale from that compendium of misinformation, Michael Denton's *Evolution: A Theory in Crisis*. The authors pretend that there is a "ladder of life," and organisms that have apparently diverged early on from this sequence are somehow frozen in time, retaining "primitive" as opposed to "advanced" features. Hence, in their view of evolution, because "fish" are supposed to have evolved into "amphibians," fishes should have cytochromes most similar to those of amphibians. Instead, *all* the tetrapod are equally distant from the fish. Of course, this is exactly what is to be expected from evolution, because the ancestors of the living fish tested diverged from those of the tetrapod, and their cytochrome evolved as those of the tetrapod were evolving along separate pathways. This is why the fish is equidistant from the tetrapod. This is also why the bacterium *Rhodospirillum* is equidistant from all the vertebrates, invertebrates, plants, and yeast tested. Not to present the standard, internally and independently consistent evolutionary explanation of these results is inexcusable and incompetent. The following page presents the same misinformation, pretending that the consistent number of differences between the cytochrome c of the carp and of the bullfrog (13), turtle (13), chicken (14), rabbit (13), and horse (13) implies that they all might have equally well diverged independently from the carp, rather than the carp having diverged independently from the tetrapod 500 million years ago.

Of Pandas and People is a tract on hard-shell fundamentalist creationism in disguise. This underlying theme never speaks its name in this tract, but it is there nonetheless. It is hard to say what is worst in this book: the misconceptions of its sub-text, the intolerance for honest science, or the incompetence with which science is presented. In any case, teachers should be warned against using this book.

This review was originally published in *Bookwatch Reviews* 2(11) in 1989, and is reprinted by permission.

Kevin Padian
Department of Integrative Biology
and Museum of Paleontology
University of California, Berkeley 94720

OF PANDAS AND PEOPLE
The Central Question of Biological Origins

Percival Davis and Dean H. Kenyon
Haughton Publishing Company
Dallas, TX (1989)

They're Here!

Several years ago, I was a witness in Arkansas testifying against a bill passed into law mandating the teaching of Biblical literalism, alongside evolution, in state schools. The ACLU brought suit on the grounds that this violated the separation of Church and State. The law was thrown out, as was right and proper, but I still remember what one of the ACLU lawyers said: "Don't think the Creationists will go away. They won't! They'll just regroup and be smarter and sneakier next time."

I am afraid the lawyer was right, as this book under review — whose title has the gall to echo a work of one of the other ACLU witnesses, Stephen Jay Gould — shows only too well. The early creationist publications were crude affairs, not the least in their physical appearance. The leader of the pack, Duane T. Gish's *Evolution, the Fossils Say No!*, may well have sold over 150,000 copies as its cover proudly proclaimed. Yet, it was a cheap-looking thing on second-rate paper with flawed print and with contents that were little better.

Now, we have *Of Pandas and People: The Central Question of Biological Origins* — clean, crisp, beautifully-illustrated, with attractive photographs. There is even the "mandatory" Gary Larson cartoon (a good one, too!). But, it is as bogus as ever, maybe even more so than were the original productions of Gish and friends. They, at least, let you know their thesis clearly — 6,000 years of Earth history, six days of Creation, and an enormous flood. In *Of Pandas and People*, the real (same old) message is carefully concealed until you are well and truly hooked. You are, as with a judicious lecture, given an apparently disinterested discussion of rival views — evolution and design (more on this latter term in a moment). You are, as in a real textbook, taken through the various branches of biological science. (This, at least, is an improvement, since previously one tended to begin and end with the fossil record.) You are, as in a scholarly text, given plausible quotes from eminent scientists in the field — Ernst Mayr and the like. You are, however, in these types of books, plunked down on the side of evangelical religion.

> Any view or theory of origins must be held in spite of unsolved problems; proponents of both views acknowledge this. Such uncertainties are part of the healthy dynamic that drives science. However, without exaggeration, there is impressive and consistent evidence, from each area we have studied, for the view that living things are the product of intelligent design.

Beneath the gloss of the text, one soon starts to turn up familiar pseudo-arguments.

Many design proponents and some evolutionists believe *Archaeopteryx* was a true bird, capable of powered flight. The fact that it possessed reptilian features not found in most other birds does not require a relationship between birds and reptiles, anymore than the duck-billed platypus, a mammal, must be related to a duck.

Well, if you believe that, you will believe anything! You might believe, for instance, that, as we read earlier in the book, Ernst Mayr thinks so poorly of the *Origin of Species* that his views merit being included in a section on "The failure of natural selection." Or you might believe that Stephen Gould and David Raup think that the fossil record gaps spell "Big Trouble" for evolutionists. Or you might believe that the molecules tell nothing of homology and evolution, as the book suggests.

This book is worthless and dishonest — but slick and appealing, so be on your guard. And, let me (for what seems the millionth time in my life) protest at the Creationists appropriating exclusively unto themselves the mantle of religion. The world of life may or may not be designed. But the argument is not that the choice is between an exclusive disjunction of evolution and design. I believe that if God chooses to do things through unbroken law, then that is God's business, not ours. What is our business is the proper use of our God-given powers of sense and reason, to follow fearlessly where the quest for truth leads. Where it does not lead is to the pages of the book *Of Pandas and People*.

This review was originally published in *Bookwatch Reviews* 2(11) in 1989, and is reprinted by permission.

Michael Ruse
Professor of Philosophy and Zoology
University of Guelph
Ontario, Canada   N1G 2W1

OF PANDAS AND PEOPLE
The Central Question of Biological Origins

Percival Davis and Dean H. Kenyon
Haughton Publishing Company
Dallas, TX (1989)

A View From the Past

Can structures such as fins, feathers, and skulls be the result of the "common engineering work of an intelligent artisan?" In answering this question, Charles Thaxton, the Academic Editor for *Of Pandas and People*, affirmatively sums up the premise of this book which is "life is like a manufactured object, the result of intelligent shaping of matter." In striving to meet the goal of presenting data "that bear on the central question of biological origins," the authors make the following assertions:

a) Messages encoded in DNA must have originated from an intelligent cause.

b) Biological structures exhibit the characteristics of manufactured things.

c) Organisms such as giraffes are a package of interrelated adaptations that has resulted from the ability and work of an intelligent designer.

d) An intelligent designer shaped clay into living forms.

e) Various forms of life began abruptly through an intelligent agency with their distinctive features (fins, feathers, etc.) already intact.

f) Similarities among living things are like preassembled units that can be plugged into a complex electronics circuit. They can be varied according to an organism's need to perform particular functions in air or water or on land. Organisms are mosaics made up from units at each biological level.

g) The fossil record is either the result of a catastrophe that followed an initial informative event or a series of informative events by an intelligent designer which matches the record of appearance found in the geological record.

h) The view of intelligent design is rooted in the observation that today human intellect is required to produce the complex arrangements of matter we see in computers, literary works, and bridges. If the present is a key to the past, then an intelligent cause similar to human intellect must have accounted for all relevantly similar complex assemblages in the past.

In assessing this list of claims and propositions, Thaxton's assertion that, "Darwin did not disprove intelligent design, he simply argued there is no need for it," seems relevant. The claim that life is the result of a design created by an intelligent cause cannot be tested and is not within the realm of science. Also, as implied by Darwin, the explanatory power and usefulness of the dicta of intelligent design in directing research and understanding the natural world make them peripheral to the study of biology. Observations of the natural world also make these dicta suspect. Stephen Jay Gould in *The Panda's Thumb* argued that, "ideal design is a lousy argument for evolution," and that, "odd arrangements and funny solutions are the proofs of evolution — paths that a sensible God would never tread but that a natural process constrained by history, follows perforce." Gould uses the orchid, which he describes as a "collection of parts generally fashioned for other purposes," and the panda's thumb, which he described as a contraption that is a modified radial sesamoid bone and anatomically not a finger, as examples that reflect evolution in nature rather than intelligent design.

In 1886, Thomas Huxley argued in his book *Lay Sermons, Addresses, and Reviews* that the hypothesis of special creation was not only a "specious mask of our ignorance" but its "existence in Biology marks the youth and imperfections of the science." Huxley indicated the history of every science involved the "elimination of the notion of creative or other interferences with the natural order of the phenomena which are subject matter of that science." He indicated that when astronomy was a young science "the morning stars sang together for joy" and the "planets were guided on their courses by celestial hands." In 1989, *Of Pandas and People* represents the continued efforts of a vanguard to keep an earlier and less mature view of the world entrenched in biology classrooms.

The view that life is the result of the design by an intelligent cause was in the mainstream of American thought as late as the nineteenth century. Prior to the Civil War, nearly ever college and university had a natural philosophy course that was built around the basic tenets presented in this book. The course was so important it generally was taught by the school's president. In the late 1800s, the faculty at Johns Hopkins University revised the biological sciences curriculum and eliminated the emphasis on creative design and other creationist tenets. Other colleges and universities eventually did likewise. These actions were not the result of censorship or abridgement of academic freedom. Creationist ideas, which were once in the center of human thought, had become fringe ideas that had no power to explain the natural world. Today, they remain fringe ideas that have no legitimate place in the study of biology beyond their historical significance as ideas that once dominated human thought.

Because of legislative and judicial setbacks in their efforts to ban the teaching of evolution or to neutralize it with equal treatment of creationism, the antievolutionists now are focusing their attack on evolution. This book reflects that strategy. Also, the antievolutionists are interpreting the statement in *Edwards v. Aguillard*, 482 U.S. 96 (1987) that indicated "teaching a variety of scientific theories about the origins of humankind to school children might be validly done with the clear secular intent of enhancing the effectiveness of science instruction" as support for the teaching of creationist tenets. Undoubtedly, the authors also were encouraged by the Texas State Board of Education's guidelines for the upcoming adoption of biology and elementary science textbooks that mandate the coverage of "scientific theories of evolution and other reliable scientific theories, if any." As stated by Robert Simonds in the creationist publication "Impact" (October, 1989), there are many school administrators, school board members, and teachers who are "closet creationists" who want to support creationist views. This book may find favor with these individuals. No one, however, should be seduced by the argument that the idea, "life is the result of an intelligent plan conceived by an intelligent agent," is a scientific theory or model, and as such, should be studied by students to balance or neutralize the teaching of evolution. Clearly, *Pandas* is being used as a vehicle to advance sectarian tenets and not to improve science education. This book has no potential to improve science education and student understanding of the natural world. Richard Dawkins in *The Blind Watchmaker* asserted that "biology is the study of complicated things that give the appearance of having been designed for a purpose" and that "all appearances to the contrary, the only watchmaker in nature is the blind forces of physics, albeit displayed in a very special way." The authors of *Pandas* have been seduced by the complicated nature of life and, undoubtedly, by other factors to see purpose and design in nature. As a result they cling to an outmoded orthodoxy that represents poor science. No benefit could be achieved by emphasizing this orthodoxy in the biology classrooms of this nation.

This review was originally published in *Bookwatch Reviews* 2(11) in 1989, and is reprinted by permission.

Gerald Skoog
President, National Science Teachers' Association, 1985-86, and
Professor of Educational Leadership and Secondary Education
Texas Tech University
Lubbock, TX 74904

EVOLUTION: A THEORY IN CRISIS

by Michael Denton
Adler & Adler
Bethesda, MD (1986)

Evolutionary biology is in robust health. The current flurry of debates is an early sign of a new burst of growth. Some observers, apparently deceived by the hyperbole that has accompanied these debates, have mistaken growth pains for terminal illness. Michael Denton is one such observer. *Evolution: A Theory in Crisis* is an anti-evolution treatise. Its theme, exemplified by the title and stated explicitly in the preface, is that there is a crisis in evolutionary biology of fatal proportions. Its parting conclusion is the fallacious assertion that the achievements of evolutionary biology amount to nothing more than "the great cosmogenic myth of the twentieth century" and provide no new insight to the origin of living beings on earth.

The book belongs to the "creation science" genre. Denton's presentation differs from the usual creation science works in only one respect: he does not actively espouse the creation science claim for a scientific basis in Genesis. The book, therefore, has the appearance of being strictly a book on biology. Intelligent laypersons reading Denton's book may think that they have encountered a scientific refutation of evolutionary biology. As a serious piece of biology, however, the book could not pass the most sympathetic peer review. In its approach, methods, and style it is straight out of the creation science mold. Abuses typical of creation science literature abound: evolutionary theory is misrepresented and distorted; spurious arguments are advanced as disproof of topics to which the arguments are, at best, tangentially relevant; evolutionary biologists are quoted out of context; large portions of relevant scientific literature are ignored; dubious or inaccurate statements appears as bald assertions accompanied, more often than not, with scorn.

Deciding how to deal with such a book is not a trivial problem. The book purports to be a biological treatise. Its scope ranges from paleontology to molecular biology, with excursions into the history and philosophy of biology. No area escapes misrepresentation and distortion. Point by point rebuttals would require a treatise of comparable proportions, which is certainly beyond the limits of any one review. Besides, detailed exposés of creation science literature already exist, including Philip Kitcher's *Abusing Science: The Case Against Creationism* (Cambridge: MIT Press, 1982) and the collection of essays, *Scientists Confront Creationism*, edited by Laurie Godfrey (NY:Norton, 1983). Many of Denton's misconceptions and distortions are addressed by these two works.

If this were simply a book written for scientists it could be ignored. However, it is not; it is clearly intended for laypersons, whose interest is most likely motivated by philosophical and theological issues. Such an audience cannot be expected to have the necessary expertise to avoid being deceived by the book's manifold abuses of evolutionary biology. A detailed critique being out of the question, the strategy adopted here is to focus upon two themes that are characteristic of the book's treatment of evolutionary biology: chance and typology.

The first theme, which occurs repeatedly as a leitmotif, is that familiar old war horse, "Mere Chance." It first appears in the preface with the statement that since Charles Darwin's time "... chance ruled supreme. God's will was replaced by the capriciousness of a roulette wheel." In a later passage is found the assertion: "The driving force behind the whole of evolution was the purely random process of natural selection" (p. 60). Equating natural selection and the origin of adaptations with "problem solving by trial and error" and "gigantic random searches" is a repeated theme (e.g., pp. 61 and 308).

Pejorative appeal to naive notions of "chance" is typical of creation science literature and is a clear sign that Denton's book is not to be taken as a serious book on biology. Describing natural selection as a purely random process distorts basic population genetic theory. Such statements demonstrate lack of understanding of Darwin's ideas and fail to acknowledge a vast amount of contemporary literature, especially the relevant writings of Ernst Mayr (who is, nevertheless, referenced sixteen times in Denton's index with respect to other topics). Nonbiologists can find a good discussion of the way in which random processes interact with deterministic processes in the theory of organic evolution through natural selection in Mayr's article "Evolution," *The Scientific American* 239 (Sept 1978):46-55.

Furthermore, the word *chance*, in its every day usage, is filled with ambiguity and imprecision. Kitcher (chap. 4) provides a good discussion of different meanings subsumed by the term, several of which commonly occur in discussions of evolution. The different usages imply very different contexts and carry very different connotations. Because stochastic processes occur in virtually every branch of science, including evolutionary biology, and because laypersons, especially those who are less comfortable with mathematics, often have difficulties with the concept of random events and with processes governed by probabilistic laws, any writer attempting a serious discussion of phenomena that involve random processes has an obligation to exercise reasonable precision in the way that the role of random events is presented. Uncritical imputation of "mere chance" is not appropriate.

The second theme, which is the major theme of the book, is a typological view of organisms. Six chapters are devoted to a resurrection of this view of biological organization. Under a typological view, different kinds of organisms are regarded as constituting distinct, independent *types* between which any concept of genealogical relatedness is meaningless. Under a typological view, variation is without significance: variations within a type are distractions, inconsequential deviations from the essence of the type; similarities (and differences) between types are mere coincidents, the by-product of each type's being what it is. Subscription to a typological view of organisms was the norm among early nineteenth-century biologists. (It is still a central tenet of current creationism. Denton's focus on typology is right in step with the creationists' agenda.) Abandonment of a typological view of organisms and recognition of the significance that individual variability has had in the history of life on earth is precisely what the Darwinian revolution was all about. In *The Genetic Basis of Evolutionary Change* (NY: Columbia Univ. Press, 1974), Richard Lewontin emphasized this point with a touch of elegance: "He [Darwin] called attention to the actual variation among actual organisms as the most essential and illuminating fact of nature. Rather than regarding the variation among members of the same species as an annoying distraction, as a shimmering of the air that distorts our view of the essential object, he made that variation the cornerstone of his theory."

When stripped of its cloak of respectable terminology, Denton's case for a typological view of organisms is seen as nothing more than the old arguments of "missing links" and "gaps in the fossil record" — arguments that long ago ceased to have biological support. Current debates among biologists on the topic of gradualism versus punctuationalism might appear to involve new evidence, but these debates are, in fact, a red herring for advocates of a typological view of organisms. The key issue for typological thinkers is an absence of genealogical relations between types. The questioning of gradualism by contemporary biologists is a debate, first, about the tempo of morphological change and, second, about processes responsible for large-scale patterns of variation among organisms. Nowhere in the debates is the issue of genealogical relatedness brought into question.

Denton attempts to build a broad case for his typological perspective. I shall confine attention to his treatments of molecular data, which his editors specifically tout in the blurbs on the dust jacket. (Readers interested in problems with Denton's treatment of other areas should see the chapters by Joel Cracraft, Laurie Godfrey, and C. Loring Brace in *Scientists Confront Creationism*.) Advances in molecular biology during the past thirty years opened a new window for viewing genealogical relations among organisms. The results are close to spectacular. Embedded in the structures of common proteins are telltale clues of genealogical relationships that provide overwhelming, independent, corroboration of the principle of biological evolution. Typological thinking in biology died long ago; molecular data have sealed the coffin. Denton, however, contends that molecular biology provides new evidence for a typological view of organisms. Inspection of Denton's arguments in Chapter 12 — "A Biochemical Echo of Typology" — reveal that his conclusions are based upon an artifact produced by faulty interpretation of the data. Since Denton's professional training is said to be in molecular biology, a detailed look at this situation is in order.

Biochemists have elucidated detailed structures of a variety of proteins obtained from a diverse array of organisms. (Anyone unfamiliar with rudimentary molecular genetics can read, with confidence, Denton's Chapter 11.) Some of the proteins studied are found only in certain kinds of organisms; others occur in virtually all organisms. In the latter case, the molecular structure of a specific protein — cytochrome C is a classic example and the one used by Denton — can be determined in each of many different organisms. It turns out that the structures of the same protein in two different organisms are rarely identical and in some cases quite dissimilar. The amount of difference can be quantified.

Denton provides representative data in Table 12.1. The data are extracted from the leading biochemical reference on the subject and are good; Denton's analysis and conclusions are not. Denton builds his arguments upon a phenomenon that he calls "molecular equidistance." He uses this phrase to refer to empirical results such as the observation that cytochrome C in bacteria, for example, differs by approximately the same amount (roughly 65-70 percent) from the cytochrome C's found in each of the other organisms listed in the table (vertebrates, insects, plants, and yeasts). Denton uses such observations to infer (erroneously) distinct typological classes. Discussing the data, he makes statements such as: "The bacterial kingdom has no neighbor in any of the fantastically diverse eukaryotic types. The 'missing links' are well and truely missing" (p. 281); and "There is not a trace at a molecular level of the traditional evolutionary series: cyclostome — fish — amphibian — reptile — mammal. Incredibly, man is as close to lamprey as are fish!" (p. 284).

These conclusions are erroneous: in his interpretation of "molecular equidistance," Denton has confused ancestor-descendant relationships with cousin relationships. The telltale clues of molecular data are not, directly, concerned with parents and offspring, intermediate forms, and "missing links." They are, instead, reflections of relative relatedness between contemporary cousins. Twentieth-century bacteria are not ancestors of twentieth-century turtles and dogs: they are very distant cousins, and, as the data in Denton's presentation show, the bacteria are roughly equally distant cousins of both turtles and dogs (and all the other organisms that Denton included in Table 12.1).

Cousin relationships between contemporary individuals are governed by the number of generations since there last was an ancestor in common to the individuals. Different members of a group of close relatives always have the same relationship to a more distantly related individual who stands outside the group. Two sisters are equally related to a mutual first cousin. Members of a group of siblings and first cousins are all equally related to a mutual fifth cousin. Lamprey are equally distant cousins of both fish and humans because the last ancestor that lampreys had in common with humans was the same ancestor lamprey had in common with fish. The "molecular equidistance" argument that Denton invokes is invalid, resulting from making comparisons between a single distantly related organism and various members of a more closely related group.

There is an irony in Denton's presentation to anyone familiar with the data of molecular evolution. Reflections of genealogical relationships are so strong in molecular data that Denton, in spite of his arguments to the contrary, is unable to hide them. The missing "trace" of which he speaks is not a trace; it is a shout. Simple inspection of the data in Table 12.1 will reveal that cytochrome C found in horses, for example, is quite similar in its molecular structure to that found in turtles, slightly less similar to that in fish, still less similar to that in insects, and very much less similar to that in bacteria. The traditional evolutionary series is very much in evidence.

Denton provides a series of diagrams (pp. 282-87) in which nested ellipses, arranged on the basis of molecular data, are used to illustrate his spurious "molecular equidistance" thesis. In these delightful figures organisms are seen to cluster fully in accord with the genealogical relationships that evolutionary biologists deduced from comparative anatomy and paleontological evidence long before molecular data were available. In the final figure, humans and chimps are seen side by side as each other's closest cousin. Anyone who wants to argue that these nested groups of organisms constitute separate, distinct, and unbridgeable groups has to contend with obvious hierarchical patterns of relatedness among the various groups. Notions of relatedness are, of course, antithetical to a typological view of organisms.

Denton claims that a crisis exists within evolutionary biology. His claim is off base: to the extent that evolutionary biology is at all involved with a crisis, the crisis lies outside of biology. For creationists, with a strictly literal interpretation of the Bible, the biological facts of human history create a theological crisis. Their assault upon sound science has elevated the American penchant for anti-intellectualism to a crisis stage with which everyone, including biologists, should be concerned. British evangelicals wrote in the 1830s that "If sound science appears to contradict the Bible, we may be sure that it is our interpretation of the Bible that is at fault" (*Christian Observer* [1832], p. 437; quoted by Stephen Neill, *Anglicanism* [Baltimore: Penguin Books, 1960], p. 240). Nevertheless, not only creationists but also many contemporary evangelical Christians are genuinely uncomfortable with evolutionary biology and what they perceive as a threat to the scriptural basis of their faith.

In other theological circles, evolutionary biology created little, if any, crisis. In 1930 William Temple, the Archbishop of York, wrote: "When my Father [Frederick Temple, Archbishop of Canterbury] announced and defended his acceptance of evolution in his Brough Lectures in 1884 it provoked no serious amount of criticism.... The particular battle over evolution was already won by 1884" (F.A. Iremonger, *William Temple, Archbishop of Canterbury, His Life and Letters* [London: Oxford Univ. Press, 1948], p. 491). To a large extent it would seem that evolution has been tacitly accepted and essentially ignored within such circles, although there has been a significant number of serious attempts to integrate evolutionary understanding into theology. Pierre Teilhard de Chardin provides a famous example, as does biologist Theodosius Dobzhansky. For more than twenty years the pages of *Zygon*, to cite an obvious example, have carried notable contributions from scientists and theologians. I suggest, however, that such efforts have been predominantly academic and philosophical. For the typical cleric and the average person in a pew on Sunday mornings, evolutionary biology, if not considered outright hostile to religious convictions, tends to be kept in a separate mental compartment.

Biology and theology each have important things to say about the human condition. Sound science without theology leaves us stranded with subjective values, no basis for morality, and no conception of purpose. Sound theology, if it ignores biology, can give at most incomplete — and at times faulty — understanding of human nature. Creationists use an objectionable piece of theology to justify inexcusably bad science. Books like *Evolution: A Theory in Crisis* are, at the very least, hindrances. We need good science and good theology. The two have operated too long in isolation. The time is ripe for a grand synthesis that will bring into register the complementary insights into human nature provided by modern biology and biblical theology.

Review originally published in *Zygon* (22)2, and reprinted by permission.

Philip T. Spieth
Associate Professor of Genetics
University of California, Berkeley 94720

FOSSILS
Hard Facts From the Earth

by Norman Fox
Creation-Life Publishers
San Diego, CA (1981)

As a scientist, I view with alarm the continued decline in science education in the United States and strongly support an increased emphasis on science at all grade levels. Such instruction should stress development of the student's ability to think critically rather than simple regurgitation of facts from memory. One way of reaching this goal is to present conflicting scientific hypotheses for discussion, but it is imperative that both hypotheses be viable scientific alternatives. Such is not the case in *Fossils: Hard Facts from the Earth*. The book is designed for use in grades 5-8. I will first address some, but not all, of its inaccuracies and deficiencies, and will conclude by considering three major areas of concern regarding the book.

Fox's definition (p. 2) of evolution as life growing "more complicated" is a poor one. "Change through time" or "descent with modification" would be better. As organisms adapt to different environments and lifestyles, they may become either more complex or more simple. Examples of the latter are the many thousands of species that are parasitic. This type of adaptation often entails reduction in size, as well as loss of wings, appendages, eyes, digestive systems, or other structures that were present in the parasites' ancestors.

The author's understanding of Precambrian paleontology appears to be severely limited. His source on the Precambrian fossil record is a paper published in 1958. Since that time our knowledge of Precambrian life has greatly increased, and the major evolutionary events are now well known (see Barghoorn 1971). Did Fox even look at the scientific literature on Precambrian life published during the last twenty years?

I take strong exception to the statement that fossil man tracks have been found with dinosaur tracks. Such "human tracks" have never been described in any legitimate scientific journal. Tracks that creationists claim are the best always seem to be "eroded away" before they can be collected. In citing an article by Roland Bird as evidence for the authenticity of certain tracks, Fox grossly misrepresents Bird's position. Nowhere in the paper does Bird state that real human footprints were discovered; he does state, however, that several of the local townspeople admitted to carving the human tracks for sale to tourists. Other creationists such as Neufeld (1975) regard these "human tracks" as forgeries and discount them. The tracks are actually eroded dinosaur tracks, erosional features, or forgeries (see Godfrey 1981, Weber 1981). In light of all this negative evidence, it is ridiculous to present these so-called human tracks as fact; and the clear misrepresentation of Bird's paper is deplorable.

Fox says (p. 8) that flooding is the most likely way for animals to become buried. This is incorrect. An examination both of the fossil record and of today's biological world will quickly show that much of the earth's biota are marine invertebrates. These aquatic animals cannot be "flooded" as they already live in water. In actual fact, marine invertebrates normally become fossilized through being buried by sediments derived from the eroding continents. Water-lain deposits do indeed often contain terrestrial vertebrates; but these deposits, with their fossils, were generally laid down by freshwater rivers, ponds, and lakes, and not by a flood. The "graveyard of fossils" which Fox eloquently describes, containing millions or billions of varied life forms, does not exist. There simply is no evidence for such a statement, and Schadewald (1982) has exposed the fraudulent nature of the claim.

Fox's description of the famous Agate Springs quarry is blatantly incorrect. The accompanying illustration shows a slab of fossil bones from an exhibit at the American Museum of Natural History. The slab, according to Fox, "contains bones of animals that would live in many different zones" (p. 12). (This assertion is intended to justify the creationist contention that the arrangement of fossils in the geological column results from hydrological and ecological sorting and mixing caused by flood waters.) Alas for the creationist case! Nearly 100% of the fossils in Fox's illustrative slab represent a single species of small rhinoceros.

Fossils: Hard Facts from the Earth states that "real strata always have gaps or reversals" in "order" (p. 13). From what we know of modern depositional environments, gaps in the geologic record are to be expected. The sedimentary record at any one spot results from normal shifting patterns of erosion and deposition. But to say that "reversals" are always present is not true. Overturned sequences do occur, but only in areas of great compressional forces such as mountain-building areas: e.g., the Alps. In sequences here, a wide variety of geologic evidence — footprints, cross bedding, graded bedding, load casts, mudcracks, etc. — will show which direction is up, and thus make the overturned nature of the sequence clear. This is quite a different matter from claiming, as Fox does, that the sequences are deposited out of order. Further, large scale thrust faulting can push older sediments over younger ones. This phenomenon is associated with large compressional forces during mountain building, and is not a reversed sequence of deposition. All this is basic physical and historical geology.

Fox states (p. 22) that "present processes do not form life from non-living things." This is true, as far as we know. However, the environment of the early earth, and the conditions under which life presumably arose, were very different from those of the present day. Thus Fox's statement is irrelevant to the discussion. Based on the geochemistry of Precambrian rock, and on what we know of planetary atmospheres, the environment of the early earth can be roughly recreated in laboratories. Under such conditions the chemical precursors of life have been produced by natural processes. For a discussion of the chemical evolution of life see Cloud (1976).

Invertebrates do not appear, as Fox suggests (p. 23), "complete and complex" at the beginning of the Cambrian. Their precursors, some quite complex, occur in Precambrian strata. Also, Cambrian invertebrate fauna are far from complete, since many higher taxonomic groups are unknown from these strata. Contrary to Fox's statements concerning vertebrate fossils, intermediate forms are known that connect the major classes of vertebrates. Examples of intermediates, and the classes that they connect, include *Ichthyostega* (fish-amphibians), *Seymouria* (amphibians-reptiles), *Archaeopteryx* (reptiles-birds), *Tritylodon* (reptiles-mammals).

Fox takes the classic creationist position that *Archaeopteryx* is not an intermediate or transitional form but is unquestionably a bird. Fox supports his argument with figures (p. 23) of *Archaeopteryx* and of a recently described "modern" contemporary. The "modern" form is apparently avian, but not even its discoverer claims that it is a modern bird — only that it could fly. The remains are diagnostic but fragmentary, consisting of a limb bone and a partial pelvis (Figure 1). Fox, however, chose to illustrate this fossil with a drawing of the complete skeleton of a modern pigeon. By captioning the pigeon "NEW FIND," Fox deceives his readers.

Fox suggests (p. 23) that some fossils "look like transitional forms" because they were created to look that way. Such reasoning conveniently explains away any evidence that contradicts the creation model; this is not scientific thinking. Fox says further that "no one has seen an organism change to a whole new kind." The argument is ludicrous. No evolutionary biologist is ever going to sit up nights hoping to get a flash shot of such an event the instant it occurs. Evolution does not involve a single organism changing into another kind of single organism. Evolution involves a whole group or a whole gene pool slowly changing into a different group or gene pool.

A "great flood" weighs heavily in Fox's defense of creationist earth history. As one line of evidence for the great flood, Fox cites (p. 24) "tall fossils extending through several layers." All such examples that I know of are trees, and the explanation is simple. Mud flows, or air-blown volcanic ash, can suddenly cover an entire forest and bury it upright. The roots are fossilized in the old soil and the trunks in the newly deposited sediments. The trees "extend through several layers." The most spectacular example of this phenomenon is in Yellowstone National Park, where 27 fossilized forests are preserved, recording the repeated burial and regrowth of the Yellowstone forests (see Dorf 1964).

Aside from the specific technical deficiencies discussed above, I have three general objections to the supposedly fair presentation of the creation-evolution dispute in the book under review. First, the treatise offers as science a theory — special creation — which has been under exhaustive examination for well over a hundred years. It has already been falsified by basic biology and geology, and has been rejected for good cause by substantially the entire world scientific community. As noted above, a universal flood — i.e., one which totally covered the earth — is central to the "creation model" as elaborated by Fox and by the Institute for Creation Research. However, the flood hypothesis is clearly falsified by a large body of geologic and biologic data. For an extended discussion of this question see publications by Gould (1982), Schadewald (1982), and Weber (1980).

A second general objection to this book is its failure to discuss radiometric dating. Indeed, the very existence of this invaluable technique for geochronology is denied on page 24, where the author writes, "No one can really measure the age of fossils for sure." Reliable dating bears directly

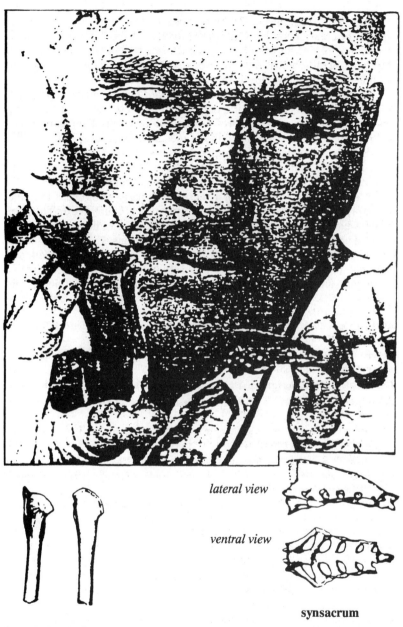

lateral view

ventral view

synsacrum

lateral view (left), ventral view (right)
tibiotarsus

Figure 1. Actual views of *Palaeopteryx*, the "modern" bird that coexisted with *Archaeopteryx*. Compare with skeleton marked "NEW FIND" in Fox's book, p. 23. Photo (top) from *BYU Today*, March 1982, p. 30. Drawings (bottom) from J.A. Jensen, *Encyclia* 58:109, 1982. By permission.

on many of the questions raised in this book, and provides critical evidence against the creation model. If the entire fossil record is the result of a single flood, then all rock layers should give the same radiometric date. Tens of thousands of radiometric dates have been obtained throughout the geologic column, and they show clearly that all deposits are not the same age.

My third general objection to *Fossils: Hard Facts* is its misrepresentation of the contents of scientific papers and its presentation of numerous unsubstantiated "facts." As a professional paleontologist I am familiar with much of the scientific literature in my specialty. In several instances Fox cites references which do not support his assertions. In other instances there is absolutely no evidence for Fox's "facts." Thus readers who are not familiar with the literature can be misled by Fox's references to it.

A science text which stimulates critical thought would be admirable; unfortunately *Fossils: Hard Facts from the Earth* is not such a text. The flood model which it supports has been decisively falsified, radiometric dating is omitted and its validity denied, scientific publications are misrepresented, and unsubstantiated "facts" are presented as valid scientific evidence. Thus the book would not contribute usefully to an acceptable scientific curriculum and I cannot recommend its use or adoption by public schools.

References

S.E. Barghoorn, 1971. "The oldest fossils." **Scientific American**. Reprinted in L.F. Laporte (ed.), 1978. **Evolution and the Fossil Record.** Freeman. pp. 44-56.

P.Cloud, 1976. "Beginnings of biosphere evolution and their biogeochemical consequences." **Paleobiology** 2(3): 351-387.

J.R. Cole, 1981. "Misquoted scientists respond." **Creation/Evolution** VI (Fall 1981):34-44.

E. Dorf, 1964. "The Petrified Forests of Yellowstone Park." **Scientific American**, April: 106-114.

L.R. Godfrey, 1981. "An analysis of the creationist film, 'Footprints in Stone'." **Creation/Evolution** VI (Fall 1981):24-29.

B. Neufeld, 1975. "Dinosaur tracks and giant men." **Origins** 2(2): 64-76.

R.J. Schadewald, 1982. "Six 'flood' arguments creationists can't answer." **Creation/Evolution** IX (Summer 1982):18-22.

C.C. Weber, 1980. "The fatal flaws of flood geology." **Creation/Evolution** I (Summer 1980):24-37.

Daniel J. Chure
Park Paleontologist
Jensen, UT 94035

The contents of this review reflect the views of Mr. Chure as a professional paleontologist and do not necessarily reflect the views of the Dinosaur National Monument, the National Park Service, or the Department of the Interior.

CREATION'S TINY MYSTERY

by Robert V. Gentry
Earth Science Associates
Knoxville, TN (2nd edition, 1988)

Earth science educators occasionally encounter students who have questions about the age of the earth, its evolution and how Polonium pleochroic halos indicate that the world was, in fact, created only 6,000 years ago. This concept is summarized by Robert V. Gentry in his book *Creation's Tiny Mystery*.

The book is in mostly an autobiography. It details the persecution that Gentry thinks he has experienced from the scientific "establishment." It is the commentary of a very sad man who was the star witness for the state of Arkansas in their defense of a suit brought by the ACLU over a law requiring the teaching of creation "science." On January 5, 1982, Judge Overton ruled against the constitutionality of this law, for which Gentry was the scientific champion. Discussions about the Arkansas trial take up 8 of the 13 chapters.

Gentry's ideas about Po haloes are based on studies which he conducted between 1966 and 1979 wherein he identified extinct radioactivity from short-lived isotopes of Po in the uranium-to-lead decay series. The existence of radio halo patterns for Po-218 (half-life 3 minutes), Po-214 (half-life 164 microseconds) are interpreted by Gentry to be evidence for instantaneous creation by God of the earth from nothing. The rocks must have formed on microseconds, not over millions of years. Otherwise the Po haloes would not survive.

Gentry's thesis has several logical flaws which have been addressed by Collins (1988), Wakefield (1988a, 1988b), Wakefield and Wilkerson (1990), and Wilkerson (1987). Geologic study of the sites where Po halo-containing specimens have been collected reveal that all are from uranium mines or rocks containing high concentrations of uranium and thorium. The pegmatites and veins that host the Po-bearing minerals cut across older rocks and the mineralization sequences in the pegmatite/veins indicate that the biotite (which generally hosts the Po haloes) are among the youngest minerals to form in these pegmatite and veins. These sites have undergone a complex (but decipherable) sequence of geologic events. These data do not support Gentry's idea of essentially instantaneous creation for the ore bodies (and by extension the earth). These geologic arguments against Gentry's creationist theory are customarily brushed aside by him and his supporters with the justification that geologists labor under the false philosophy of uniformitarianism. Indeed, Gentry has many uncomplimentary things to say about geologists and in his book. Most of this is due to religious presuppositions but also to a very poor understanding of how geologists work nowadays.

From the standpoint of an educator, Gentry's book would be of interest only as a classic example of religious zeal and its results on a quest for scientific knowledge. I cannot recommend it as a science text, although it is unique in having a catalogue of photographs of different types of haloes.

Sociologists or psychologists (or theologians!) could probably find the seeds of several Ph.D theses in it. (How odd that God would put these microscopic petrographic structures in ancient rocks of the earth's crust in order to have a prophet-scientist popularize them as evidence for divine action.)

Although Gentry does not say so, his activities are very much influenced by his dedication to the writings of Ellen G. White and traditions of the Seventh Day Adventist church. Interestingly enough, the scientific arm of the Adventist church, the Geoscience Research Institute at Loma Linda University has rejected Gentry's work (Brown et al. 1988).

In summary, there is nothing that Gentry has observed in Po haloes that cannot be explained in terms of modern geologic theory. They do *not* give unequivocal evidence for fiat creation. The book is a source of much misinformation about current geologic thinking and confuses fact with interpretation at several points. In general I don't think educators will find it worth their time to tread through this creationist's whining.

References

Brown, R.H, H.G. Coffin, L.J. Gibson, A.A. Roth and C.L. Webster 1988. "Examining Radiohalos." **Origins** 15(1).

Collins, L.G. 1988. **Hydrothermal Differentiation and Myremekite: A clue to many geologic puzzles.** Athens, Greece: Theophrastus Publications.

Wakefield, R. 1988a. "Gentry's Tiny Mystery — Unsupported by Geology." **Creation/Evolution** 22:13-33.

Wakefield, R. 1988b. "The Geology of Gentry's 'Tiny Mystery'." **Journal of Geologic Education** 36:161-175.

Wakefield, R. and G. Wilkerson 1990. "Geologic Setting of Polonium Radiohalos." **Proceedings of the Second International Conference on Creationism**, Volume II. Pittsburgh, PA: Creation Science Fellowship, Inc., pp.329-343.

Wilkerson, G. 1987. "Po Haloes, Arkansas Creation-Evolution Trial and an Autobiography: Book Review of Creation's Tiny Mystery, Gentry 1986." **Origins Research** 10(1):10-11.

Gregg Wilkerson, Ph.D.
Geologist
Bureau of Land Management
Bakersfield, CA 93301

The contents of this review reflect the views of Dr. Wilkerson as a professional geologist and do not necessarily reflect the views of the Bureau of Land Management.

EVOLUTION
The Challenge of the Fossil Record
by Duane T. Gish
Creation-Life Publishers
El Cajon, CA (1985)

This is an updated version of Gish's two best-sellers, *Evolution: The Fossils Say NO!* (regular edition and public school version). The updating is cosmetic. The new subtitle takes even more chutzpa than the first version's, since the fossil record is such a challenge to creationism. But the fossil record is indeed Gish's focus in this as well as the earlier editions.

It is daunting to try to review a book which is rife with error and misunderstanding on every page. Using a veritable avalanche of factoids, the author tries to convince the reader that a sound case is being made — no one has the energy to dissect the book, line by line. Certainly, I don't! (A thorough "review" of this laundry-list of claims and assertions is, in a way, the mission-impossible of *Creation/Evolution* journal and various book-length critiques of scientific creationism (see Appendix).) A second Gish tactic is to cite a respected scientific position and simply declare it wrong.

Let me choose random pages. On page 80, Gish cites an interview with scholars about fossil cetaceans and then asks questions about topics that weren't covered: Were the bones all from one individual? Even the same species? The paleontologists could have answered these and other questions, but they were asked rhetorically by Gish, not by the original interviewer, so scientists are recorded as mute on such questions. Gish happily quotes bits and pieces of various evolutionists' writings, as before. He "explains" that radiometric dating just doesn't work. He harps on the supposed absence of transitional fossils, even while listing a few of them. For example, australopithecines, "Java Man" and "Peking Man" are dismissed as apes, while Neanderthals are called fully modern (pp. 203 ff.). Gish also repeats the claim that all "Peking Man" remains are lost and only known by hearsay; in fact, a number of specimens have been found since World War II at the same site near Peking, and the "lost" fossils were carefully photographed, measured, and documented. According to Gish, *Archaeopteryx* is just a bird (p. 110) or just reptile (pp. 110-111), not transitional. Thus (typically), fossils which contradict Gish's claims are used as if they prove him right.

Gish cites allegedly contradictory dates for various fossils and various strata, and concludes that since scientists can't agree on anything, he'll step in with his "better" explanation. But, as usual, he picks and chooses his strawmen to attack and then flails away with his "simple solution." He wrongly equates "catastrophism" with "creationism" in order to claim the scientific credentials of catastrophism (new and old). Any disagreements with natural selection, the modern synthesis, or any specific fossil or geological detail become, in Gish's hands, attacks on the whole fabric of evolutionary theories and *de facto* support for creationism, which he falsely treats as the only alternative to evolution. Gish misconstrues statements by

Gould, Simpson, Stanley, Raup, and many others — even though by the time this "new" edition was published he had been corrected in person and in print, so ignorance is no excuse (if it ever was). Page after page, Gish summons up examples of this and that researcher and then dismisses them as simply wrong, implying that anyone with half a brain could recognize this for themselves. He uses a sort of inverted appeal to authority, by showing how silly and pointless is the life work of each scholar cited. He feigns complex understanding by using strings of complicated words ("meningocele, spina bifida, chondrodystrophy, cleft palate, hemangiomas, syndactyly, hypodactyly, and heterotrophic anus," for example, on page 220 — a list of birth defects which is quite daunting to see, however meaningless to any argument being made).

In this book, Gish writes about origins of races, languages, "tribes," etc. from the eight survivors of Noah's ark; discusses where Cain and Abel got wives; and otherwise deals with Biblical issues more openly than in the "public school" version of his earlier book.

The first versions of this book are among the most widely quoted creationist sources, and this version may catch up, given time. Unless you're a debater, though, you probably don't need a copy of this rehash if you already have the original hash. But if you are involved in science or religious education in any way, you should read one of these Gish books if you want to understand what arguments teachers, scientists and theologians face in classrooms and churches.

John R. Cole, Ph.D.
Board of Directors
National Center for Science Education, Inc., and
Water Resources Research Center
University of Massachusetts
Amherst, MA 01003

THE EARTH IS NOT MOVING

by Marshall Hall
Fair Education Foundation
Athens, GA (1991)

When "scientific creationism" first made its presence felt in the U.S. court system, a number of political cartoonists depicted that next a motionless Earth would be introduced, as a humorous example of American science education going backwards into the Dark Ages. Their lampoon was prophetic, with the publication of Hall's *The Earth Is Not Moving*, the latest in a group of books which seeks to establish "Biblical astronomy" (i.e. geocentrism).

Whereas Dr. Gerardus Bouw's geocentrism book, *With Every Wind of Doctrine*, was a detailed literalist's catalog of Biblical geocentrist verses and their interpretation in a geocentrist way (plus some beatification of Tycho thrown in), and Van der Kamp's *De Labore Solis* was an affected pseudo-philosophical stab at Copernican underpinnings, Hall has written for the vast audience of people who take their Bibles literally – but not too carefully – and who also do not understand much (if any) physics. Acceptance of Hall's thesis is also enhanced if the reader is distrustful of science.

In brief, Hall considers Copernicanism a Satanic Lie, and does not shy away from saying this over and over. Indeed, "lie" is one of the most extensively used words in the volume, capitalized and uncapitalized. Under "Einstein" we find: "As a Zionist Jew, Einstein was an implacable enemy of Jesus Christ and His New Testament. That New Testament says plainly that all who deny that Jesus has come in the flesh as the Son of God are liars and anti-Christs." He also claims that, "Einstein is one of the most outstanding figures in world history because he accomplished a task that Satan has been working on for centuries," and reports, almost verbatim, a story originated by the Nazi, Lenard, of how Einstein's ideas were plagiarized. In the chapter, "Kepler: The Witchcraft Connection," we find the statement, "Mr. Kepler was a demon-led loonie bird." Quoting Kepler's First Law, Hall comments: "'The planets move around the sun in ellipses having the sun at one of the foci.' Foci. Schmoki. Loci. Poci. If the sun is one of the foci, wonder what the other foci is, er ah, are?" [sic]

Whereas previous geocentrists have used pieces of scientific theories to explain their pseudoscience, such as Bouw's using the Coriolis Effect as a real force caused by a rotating Universe, Hall dismisses all of the proofs of a moving Earth as lies with statements such as, "The Coriolis Effect is a demonstrable reality which results when something is in motion over a rotating base. But applying this demonstrable reality to the Earth which has never been shown to be moving is a contra-scientific deception!" and "It is He and His Word that the Foucault Pendulum calls a liar!" Hall also denies almost every other proof, such as the existence of an equatorial bulge, in spite of the fact that every surveyor must correct for the differences between geographical and geocentric latitude (which is caused by the oblateness of the Earth's shape).

This is the flavor of the whole book. "The enormous deceptions of heliocentricity and evolutionism are like two great flood gates that contain a hidden lake full of Satan's deceptions!"

And yet, in spite of his professed disdain for lies, Hall tells a few himself, such as on page 42: "In fact, although scarcely anyone knows it, Brahe's non-moving earth model is used today in all the applied sciences including practical astronomy, space travel, and eclipse predictions." All of the space travel programming I've seen uses Newton's Laws, which certainly do allow for a moving Earth. One of the more popular orbital mechanics programs used in the space industry is the PC-compatible "Orbit View" from Cygnus Engineering. Order their demo disk and watch the Earth rotate.

On page 160, in a section called "The Coriolis Flim-Flam" we find that, "Gravity exerts a force of about fourteen point something pounds per square inch at the most." It is clear that Hall doesn't understand the most elementary physics and is really deceiving himself to imagine that he can write a critique of it. But he seems not to bother to understand anything that must be a "lie," for on page 161 he admits, "This kind of stuff gets too heavy for my brain otherwise."

Hall's advocacy is firmly rooted in the Biblical literalism of Joshua 10, Psalm 93, and other geocentric Bible verses, for he says, "... the whole purpose of this book is to show that the Scriptures tell the truth on this subject (and by extension all subjects!)." Then he quotes Psalm 19:

> In them [the firmament] hath He set a tabernacle for the sun, which is as a bridegroom coming out of his chamber, and rejoiceth as a strong man to run a race. His going forth is from the end of heaven, and his circuit into the ends of it.

To this Hall comments, "OK. I've got the picture. The Bible teaches that the Earth is hung on nothing, that it is fixed in a certain spot and cannot be moved, and that the sun goes around it in an orbit every day."

But that's not what Psalm 19 says. What about the "tabernacle" that the sun comes out of? Where is it? Hall doesn't explain, for like all of the heliocentric Christians he condemns as Satan's tools, he also compromises the Bible to suit his Tychonic model fancy. As Schadewald pointed out in a series of two articles in the *Bulletin of the Tychonic Society*, the Bible favors a flat-Earth model with this verse, and the sun hides in the tabernacle to explain night on the flat Earth. But then, maybe Psalm 19 is just poetic. But either there is a tabernacle for the sun or there is not.

In Hall's chapter, "Mathematics — Liar in Truth's Clothing," he recounts the torture In Orwell's 1984 where the torturer, O'Brien, held up four fingers and demanded that his victim, Winston, see five. In the same Torture session in 1984 is a passage conveniently omitted by Hall:

> "What are the stars?" said O'Brien indifferently. "They are bits of fire a few kilometers away. The Earth is the center of the Universe. The sun and stars go around it.
> "For certain purposes, of course, that is not true. When we navigate the ocean, or when we predict an eclipse, we often find it

convenient to assume the Earth goes round the sun and that the stars are millions upon millions of kilometers away. But what of it? Do you suppose it is beyond us to produce a dual system of astronomy? The stars can be near or distant, according as we need them ... Have you forgotten doublethink?"

And doublethink is precisely the fate of millions of American children indoctrinated to the nonsense of "scientific" creationism and Biblical astronomy and then asked to perform as biologists, biotechnicians, geologists, virologists, surveyors, astrophysicists, physicists and engineers. Do we want a population like that?

In spite of all the negative things about the book, or rather because of them, I actually recommend Hall's book as a warning to every astronomer and scientist concerned with public support for the sciences, for the Dark Ages are back.

Francis G. Graham
Astronomy
Kent State University
Kent, OH 44242

THE LIE: EVOLUTION

by Kenneth A. Ham
Creation-Life Publishers
Master Books Division
El Cajon, CA (1987)

One characteristic of the so-called "scientific" creationism movement is that it has produced numerous books purporting to make a scientific case against evolution and for special creation, keeping covert their purely religious underpinnings. But Ken Ham's *The Lie* is not such a book, as it makes no pretense of presenting a scientific case. The author presents an overtly *religious* case against evolution and for special creation *à la* literally read Genesis. This is not to say the author acknowledges that the great preponderance of current scientific knowledge bearing on the question of earth and life's natural history corroborates a long and evolutionary one, for Ham does no such thing, believing instead that "true" scientific knowledge does refute evolution and support biblical creation. But the explicit goal of his book is to make a religious argument, not a scientific one, and in presenting that argument Ham employs numerous anecdotes from his own and others' experiences, and he cites Bible scripture throughout.

In Chapter 1, "Christianity Under Attack," the author says that society is becoming more anti-Christian, and that today religious tolerance "really means an *intolerance of the absolutes of Christianity*" (p. 3, emphasis in original). He argues that scientists are biased, subjective humans and implies that evolutionist scientists are atheists. He says that:

> Evolution is a religious position that makes human opinion supreme. As we shall see, its fruits (because of rejection of the Creator and Lawgiver) are lawlessness, immorality, impurity, abortion, racism and a mocking of God. Creation is a religious position based on the Word of God, and it's fruits (through God's Spirit) are love, joy, peace, patience, kindness, goodness, faithfulness, gentleness and self-control. The creation/evolution issue (is God Creator?) is the crux of the problem in our society today. It is a fundamental issue with which Christians must come to grips. The creation/ evolution issue is where the battle really rages.

The author evidently regards a law-abiding, ethical, high-minded, pro-life, anti-segregationist, prayerfully reverent evolutionist to be an impossible contradiction in terms. Ham sees evolution to be one side of a simple dichotomy, God *or* evolution. He rules out (but doesn't explain why until his Appendix 1) a third possibility, God *and* evolution (which he refers to as "theistic evolution" whether "hands on" or "hand off") because (p. 154):

> In reality, theistic evolution is no different from atheistic evolution. God is simply added to the story. Christians who believe God used evolution accept what the atheistic view tells them, and then add God to the situation and reinterpret that Bible.

Clearly Ham does not allow that the idea of biological evolution springs objectively from the data of empirical science and natural history, but rather from atheism pure and simple.

In Chapter 2, "Evolution is Religion," Ham says that since the majority of evolutionists are not Christians, the term "evolutionist" should be understood to refer to people who do not regard God to be responsible for life. This falsely implies that there are few if any Christians who accept the validity of an evolutionary natural history of life. He says that evolution is basically a religious philosophy and therefore that the creation/evolution controversy is one not of science versus religion but religion versus religion.

Ham says that all evidence including fossil evidence exists in the present and implies therefore that no evidence can tell us hardly anything useful about the past. He says (p. 17, emphasis in original):

It only takes common sense to understand that one does not dig up an 'age of dinosaurs' supposedly existing 70-200 million years ago. One digs up *dead* dinosaurs that exist *now, not* millions of years ago.

He thus implies that it is only the religious aspect of evolution that imagines the natural history of life on earth to span millions of years into the past, since evolution requires great time-spans to have occurred.

Ham says (rightly!) that scientific conclusions from data can never be certainly correct, implying (wrongly!) that science and evolution scientists claim their conclusions from data to be certainly correct, which he says demonstrates that evolution is a religion. If it were true that evolutionists hold their scientific conclusions to be certainly and for all-time correct, then Ham's contention that evolution constitutes religion would be correct; but they don't, and so it isn't.

In Chapter 3, "Creation is Religion," Ham goes much further than simply acknowledging that creation is religion; he writes (p. 24):

We Christians must build all of our thinking in every area on the Bible. We must start with God's word, not the word of finite, fallible man. We must judge what people say on the basis of what God's Word says — not the other way around.

This suggests that, by Ham's logic, *everything* must be religion. Human epistemology must yield to scriptural revelation. He says that since in relation to the past nothing can be proven, neither creation nor evolution can be scientific and both are religion. He overlooks the distinction that can be made between evolution and creation, in that if evolution did not actually occur in the past, it is possible at least in principle that empirical data could demonstrate beyond reasonable doubt that evolution did not actually occur, whereas no amount of empirical data could rule out creation via supernatural God. And that distinction is the vital one that makes biological evolution scientific and creation strictly religious.

In Chapter 4, "The Root of the Problem," Ham says the real reason evolutionists don't want to admit that evolution is a religion is because evolutionists are really just people in rebellion against God who need evolution in order to justify their rebellion. In Chapter 5, "Crumbling

Foundations," Ham argues that Genesis is the very foundation of Christianity, and that "theistic evolution" insidiously attacks Genesis with the goal of destroying the foundations of Christianity, and thus ultimately Christianity entirely. Both chapters feature Ham's opinions, interpretations and Bible- based theology and contain no scientific points worthy of comment here. The same is true of chapters 6, "Genesis Does Matter," and 7, "Death — A Curse and a Blessing," in which Ham further refines his argument that the Genesis story of creation is the very foundation of all Christianity.

In Chapter 8, "The Evils of Evolution," Ham argues that abortion, pornography, homosexuality, lawlessness, Nazism, racism, drug abuse, male chauvinism and humanism are all founded on evolution, a great lie that serves Satan in a war with Christendom. He says that today's "respectability of abortion" comes from Ernst Haeckel's theory of "embryonic capitulation," which was based on data that Haeckel admitted was fraudulent but which Ham says "is still taught in many universities, schools and colleges throughout the world" (p. 89). Haeckel's theory was that the embryos of organisms go through the adult stages of all of primitive its evolutionary ancestors; his theory is in scientific disrepute and this reviewer is unaware of any universities or colleges that still teach it.

Chapters 9, "Evangelism in a Pagan World," 10, "Wake Up, Shepherds," and 11, "Creation, Flood, and Coming Fire," all constitute a religious call to evangelism and to the embracing of the Bible as the one inerrant source of truth in God's created world. Chapter 11 features evolutionists as continuing purveyors of the lie of evolution to divert people from the truth of the approaching "Last Days of earth." The only remotely scientific discussion is on page 126 where in a footnote Ham say that modern geologists have come to acknowledge that catastrophic processes have played an important role in shaping the earth's geology "in recent years, partly because of the success of creationist geologists in pointing out the clear evidence of rapid processes in the rocks." Here Ham (as have so many other so-called "scientific" creationists) mistakes "uniformitarianism" to be about *uniform rates* of processes rather than about the uniformity over time of the laws of physics governing processes. Virtually all geologists have recognized the role of catastrophes in shaping the earth's geology. Ham would have his readers believe that evolutionists deny the geologic record contains evidence of catastrophic process; it does, and all geologists acknowledge that it does. The issue is about whether a *single worldwide* flood catastrophe ever occurred, and regarding that, modern geology knows nothing.

Ham (p. 123) cites scripture and invokes Bible prophecy to explain that the reason scientists say things like modern geology knows nothing of any single worldwide flood is *not* on the basis of an absent empirical case but rather as a deliberate act of "willful ignorance" dictated under the religion of evolution.

Ham closes his last chapter by again citing prophecy for the biblical Last Days and the destruction of the earth by God which he says "we are seeing fulfilled before our very eyes," and makes a final plea for evangelism.

Following Chapter 11 there is a descriptive bibliography of other creationist publications titled "Resources." And then there are two appendices, the first titled "Twenty Reasons Why Genesis And Evolution Do Not

Mix" which offers the promised 20 thumbnail defenses of literally read Genesis as truth inviolable, and the second titled "Why did God take Six Days?" which presents a theological defense for interpreting the Genesis six days of creation literally as six 24-hour days. Almost nothing scientific is presented in these.

In summary, there is very little science presented in Ken Ham's book *The Lie*; what little there is is flawed in a number of fairly obvious ways, rendering it unsuitable for use in public school science classes. In fairness, the author would likely not protest since his book does not presume to make a scientific case for anything and is instead honest in making an overtly religious case against evolution and for special creation (which of course even further disqualifies it for use in public school science classes).

How successfully does *The Lie* make a religious case against evolution and for special creation? While the book provides a very insightful glimpse into the mind of the Bible fundamentalist, this reviewer suspects that it has very little theological merit, but leaves that judgment for readers of Ham's book to make for themselves. Many "scientific" creationists often speak the virtues of a "balanced view," so those who want to read *The Lie* in order to weigh the theological merits of Ham's religious case against evolution might want also to read *Is God a Creationist? The Religious Case Against Creation-Science* (Roland Mushat Frye, ed., Charles Scribner's Sons, New York, 1983) in order to obtain a balanced view.

Frank Lovell
Kentucky Creation/Evolution Committee of Correspondence
Chemist/Manager
Louisville, KY 40205

THE CASE FOR CREATIONISM
Fallacies of Evolution

by Arlie J. Hoover
Baker Book House
Grand Rapids, MI (1977)

Fallacies of Evolution repeatedly claims to treat in a nonemotional manner the fallacies of teaching only evolution. In the introduction, Hoover, who is Dean of Columbia Christian College in Portland, Oregon, states that he has "written a 'little book' in hopes that the public will rise up and demand equality in the teaching of origins" — meaning equality between evolution and creationism. The author labels educators who fail to accept alternatives to evolution as "no better than (educators in) Nazi Germany or Soviet Russia in their educational philosophy." Hoover says that evolutionists are guilty of a great number of fallacies, which he proceeds to list and describe. The fallacy of scientism, he says, springs from assuming "that all true knowledge is empirical, that all judgements are merely factual." Instead, Hoover believes that teachers and scientists should embrace the unseen spiritual and metaphysical world in their quest for evolutionary answers.

The chapter on special pleading by evolutionists uses emotional and inflammatory phrases to point out the shortfalls of evolution. The section on comparative anatomy is heavy with emotional terms and short, nonsensical analogies that have no real relationship to the study of anatomy. The author describes how for a long time evolutionists have been drawing charts of "similar features" of animals, for example, skeletons. "The evolutionists have constructed impressive 'ladders of life' to show the alleged orderly progression from simple to complex." But Hoover professes to use the features of a platypus as more than enough evidence to refute the use of comparative anatomy as evidence of evolution. In the section on comparative embryology the argument centers on the fact that gill pouches in the human embryo never become functioning gills, and therefore recapitulation is invalid. Ridicule of these ancient arguments is the basis of Hoover's attack on evolution.

A chapter called "What Should We Teach" presents arguments for teaching creationism in public schools. The principal argument is the syllogism: "If creation occurred we would be here. We are here. Therefore creation has occurred." This gem approximately indicates the depth of Hoover's logical and scientific profundity.

The most objectionable part of Hoover's "little book" is a chapter called "Social Darwinism and the Genetic Fallacy," in which evolution and those who subscribe to the theory become whipping boys for all of society's ills. Thus laissez-faire capitalism and imperialism are partially attributed to acceptance of Darwinism both by governments and by the earlier financial community. Also, according to Hoover, proponents of war depend on social Darwinism to justify military struggles among nations, and racists depend on it to justify the "gospel" of racial and ethnic superiority. Hoover quotes Spencer, Nietzsche, and Hitler to make these points. The view that

Hoover describes did indeed at one time have some scientific support; but social Darwinism has long been discarded by competent evolutionary biologists and anthropologists as a gross and false distortion of Darwin's ideas.

Hoover concludes his work with a plea to taxpayers to rise up against "Scientific Humanism" with its purported exclusive, prejudiced, anti-religious concrete, rational, or in-depth reasons for the rejection of evolution and the acceptance of the Biblical concept of origins. Hoover's work is full of meaningless anecdotes, emotionalism, and defamatory phraseology. The work is indeed, as the author calls it, a "little book," especially in its scientific value. Because of both its tone and its content, the book is unsuitable for public school use.

William A. Forsee
Biology teacher,
Abraham Lincoln High School
Council Bluffs, IA 51501

THE COLLAPSE OF EVOLUTION

by Scott M. Huse
Baker Book House
Grand Rapids, MI (1983)

In his Forward to *The Collapse of Evolution* the author says:

> The purpose of this book is basically three-fold: first, to expose the scientific fallacies of the theory of organic evolution; second, to present scientific evidence for Biblical creationism; and third, to prove that evolution and Biblical creationism are mutually exclusive and cannot be reconciled.

Thus, this book purports to present a *scientific* treatment, at least in accomplishing the first two folds of its three-fold purpose. Also, I learned of this book when a respected professor of medicine who regarded the book as presenting a compelling scientific treatment gave me a copy and urged me to read it, that I might learn the scientific case against evolution. And so when I began reading it I expected (as I think any reader would) to encounter in it abundant compelling scientific evidence and logical scientific arguments for the collapse of evolution as accepted scientific theory.

But that is not what I found in it. Instead, I encountered misconceptions and misrepresentations of science and of evolution theory; arguments based on long outdated data; a fictitious account of an event; a quote from an historic evolutionist that had been edited in a way that completely misrepresented the position he had written to convey. And I found an editorial slant towards creationism and against evolution so extreme that it pervaded even the book's Glossary appendix (which in most books can ordinarily be counted on to be informationally objective and free of editorializing). Space here allows me only to scratch the surface of all that I found wrong in this book, so here follows just a few examples.

Obsolete and Misrepresented Data

On page 22 Huse makes this argument for a young earth based on meteoritic dust infall from space:

> Scientists have known for some time now that cosmic dust particles enter the earth's atmosphere from space at an essentially constant rate. Eventually these dust particles settle down to the earth's surface. Hans Petterson [*sic*] has made accurate measurements of this influx, and has determined that the earth receives about 14 million tons per year. Now, if it is true that the earth is around 5 billion years old, as evolutionists insist, there should be a layer of meteoritic dust that is about 182 feet thick all over the world!

It is easy to see how this might strike a reader as a compelling scientific argument for a young earth. However, Hans Pettersson did *not* "accurately measure cosmic dust influx." He *estimated* the influx from *indirect* measurements of high altitude atmospheric particulates (whose origins are both cosmic and terrestrial), and in his original article (1) Pettersson acknowledged that his estimate involved a number of assumptions and uncertainties and that estimates of cosmic dust influx to earth made by other indirect methods were much lower than his. Yet Huse presents Pettersson's tentatively qualified estimate as if it were highly accurate and scientifically conclusive!

More important, Huse published his book 23 years after Pettersson published his infall estimates; in the decade that followed Pettersson's article, artificial earth satellites became abundant and Pettersson's data were superseded by *direct* measurements of cosmic dust in the earth's vicinity. Based on these more accurate direct measurements of cosmic dust, the current background cosmic dust infall rate is now accepted to be only about 23 thousand tons a year. This rate, made available to the public 11 years before Huse published (2), is about 1000 times lower than the rate Huse presents.

Huse mentions Pettersson's work, but he does not give a reference citation for Pettersson or to the scientific literature; instead he footnotes a book written seven years earlier by another creationist (Morris' *Scientific Creationism*).

Fictitious Account

On page 98 Huse writes:

The evidence for Nebraska Man was used by evolutionists in the famous Scopes evolution trial in Dayton, Tennessee in 1925. William Jennings Bryan was confronted with a battery of "great scientific experts" who stunned him with the "facts" of Nebraska Man. Mr. Bryan had no retort except to say that he thought the evidence was too scanty and to plead for more time. Naturally, the "experts" scoffed and made a mockery out of him. After all, who was he to question the world's greatest scientific authorities?

Huse gives no reference citation for this compelling little story, and small wonder; it is *entirely fiction!* Many scientists were all along skeptical of the validity of the "Nebraska Man" fossil and it was never widely accepted within the scientific community. Most telling, "Nebraska Man" was neither entered as evidence nor even discussed in the Scopes trial! And even if it had been, Bryan could hardly have been "stunned" by it since he already knew of it and had publicly made fun of it before the beginning of the trial (3).

Erroneous Scientific Information

Beginning on page 19, Huse offers this statement as though it represents currently accepted science:

Radioactive decay is also known to be proportional to the speed of light, and Barry Setterfield has recently shown that the speed of light has not remained fixed but has actually decreased. This decrease in the speed of light suggests that the decay of radioactive material in the rocks in the past would be much greater than it is today. Thus, the high decay rates of the past would account for the apparent vast age of the rocks.

The problem here is that the scientific literature knows nothing about "radioactive decay [being] proportional to the speed of light"; the assertion is false, and as it is stated really doesn't even make sense (the *rate* of any particular radioactive decay process is proportional to the amount of radioactive material present, not to the speed of light). Moreover, the assertion that the speed of light has been shown to have slowed over time is presently disputed by virtually all physicists including the faculty physicist of North America's premier "scientific" creationist organization, the Institute for Creation Research (4).

Misinformation

Three examples of definitions Huse gives in his Glossary (Appendix D) illustrate a lack of concern for objectivity and accuracy in the definitions that are given:

adaptation - an imagined evolutionary process through which an organism acquires characteristics which make it better suited to live and reproduce in its environment. [p. 142]

First, an "adaptation" is not a "process," it is a structure or behavior useful to an organism in a particular environment. Second, neither are adaptations "imagined," they've been recognized and called "adaptations" since long before Darwin. Perhaps Huse meant to refer to "adaptive radiation," which *is* a process, one Huse may regard to be "imaginary" but which virtually all life scientists presently regard as very much a real evolutionary process.

Archaeopteryx - A famous fossil of an extinct bird once believed by evolutionists to be a transitional form between reptiles and birds. [p. 142]

The problem with this is that *Archaeopteryx* is *still* regarded by the community of paleontologists to be a transitional form between earlier reptiles (dinosaurs) and later birds! Further, *Archaeopteryx* is not a "fossil," it is an *animal* (though granted, a "famous" and extinct animal) of which a number of fossils have now been discovered.

Numerous definitions in Huse's Glossary are inaccurate or misleadingly editorialized in the way that these are. If one's glossary is populated with erroneous *straw man* definitions of the processes and concepts of evolution and of the evidence scientists regard to support them, it is easy to at least *appear* to dispatch evolution in one's treatise. The next example will make this point without requiring further comment from this reviewer:

evolution - An imaginary process by which nature is said to continually improve itself through gradual development. (p. 146)

Incomplete (Thus Misleading) Quote

On page 73, in trying to persuade his readers of the impossibility of the evolution of the eye, Huse offers this:

.Charles Darwin acknowledged the utter inadequacy of the evolutionary theory when attempting to account for a structure such as the eye:

70

> To suppose that the eye, with all its inimitable contrivances for adjusting the focus to different distances, for admitting different amounts of light, and for the correction of spherical and chromatic aberration, could have been formed by natural selection, seems, I freely confess, absurd in the highest possible degree... The belief that an organ as perfect as the eye could have formed by natural selection is more than enough to stagger anyone.

This seems powerful testimony indeed; why, even Charles Darwin admits the great difficulty of believing that the eye could have evolved! Huse doubtless thought this quote would impress his readers, and as written I too expect that it will. But let's look at the full Darwin quote, highlighting in italics the portion omitted by the ellipsis in Huse's presentation of it:

> *Organs of extreme perfection and complication.* To suppose that the eye, with all its inimitable contrivances for adjusting the focus to different distances, for admitting different amounts of light, and for the correction of spherical and chromatic aberration, could have been formed by natural selection, seems, I freely confess, absurd in the highest possible degree. *Yet reason tells me, that if numerous gradations from a perfect and complex eye to one very imperfect and simple, each grade being useful to its possessor, can be shown to exist: if further, the eye does vary ever so slightly, and the variations be inherited, which is certainly the case; and if any variation or modification in the organ be ever useful to an animal under changing conditions of life, then the difficulty of believing that a perfect and complex eye could be formed by natural selection, though insuperable by our imagination, can hardly be considered real. How a nerve comes to be sensitive to light, hardly concerns us more than how life itself first originated; but I may remark that several facts make me suspect that any sensitive nerve may be rendered sensitive to light, and likewise to those coarser vibrations of the air which produce sound....*
>
> [Charles Darwin, *The Origin of Species*, chap. 6]

Darwin was not acknowledging "the utter inadequacy" of anything after all, but only acknowledging the difficulty one will see when first confronted with the idea that natural selection could evolve an eye; a difficulty which "can hardly be considered real" (Darwin went on to explain) after one reflects on the possibility that the eye did not evolve all at once but rather through a long series of lesser eyes (many today represented in nature) whose variations are inherited and selected over time. Huse's use of the edited Darwin quote completely misrepresents and shields his readers from Darwin's actual position regarding the feasibility of the eye as a product of evolution.

To be fair, Huse gives as a reference for his Darwin quote another creationist book rather than Darwin's book *The Origin of Species* from which the quote originates, and so the editing of the quote may not be his but rather that of the creationist in whom Huse misplaced his trust. Either way, Huse's presenting of the edited version of what Darwin wrote is a stunning example of the kinds of errors and egregious scholarship *The Collapse of Evolution* contains.

Conclusion

In delivering on the author's stated objectives of exposing the scientific fallacies of the theory of organic evolution and presenting scientific evidence for Biblical creationism, *The Collapse of Evolution* fails completely. While the book has a sufficient appearance of scholarship and contains enough scientific jargon to persuade many readers who are not trained in science (and at least one respected professor of medicine who has had scientific training), when examined closely it is revealed to be a scientifically flawed exposition that is totally unconcerned with scholarship and objectivity and is filled throughout with errors of fact and logic. The book can provide great insight into the nature and working methods of many of the so-called "scientific" creationists, but no insight whatever into the workings of nature and methods of science. For this reason *The Collapse of Evolution* cannot be recommended for use in public school science classes, nor even for independent scientific studies.

Regarding the author's objective of proving "that evolution and Biblical creationism are mutually exclusive and cannot be reconciled," this reviewer has no comment to make except to say that in trying to accomplish this objective the book contains at least 90 references to or quotes of 71 different Bible verses scattered throughout the book's 172 pages. The inclusion of this religious material constitutes an additional reason why *The Collapse of Evolution* cannot be recommended for use in public school science classes.

References

1. Pettersson, Hans 1960. "Cosmic Spherules and Meteoritic Dust." **Scientific American** 202(2):99-116.

2. Dohnanyi, J.S. 1972. "Interplanetary Objects in Review: Statistics of their Masses and Dynamics." **Icarus** 17:1-48.

3. Wolf, John and James S. Mellett 1985. "The Role Of 'Nebraska Man' in the Creation-Evolution Debate." **Creation/Evolution** 5(2):31-43.

4. Aardsma, Gerald 1988. "Has The Speed Of Light Decayed?" Institute for Creation Research **Impact** No. 179.

Frank Lovell
Kentucky Creation/Evolution Committee of Correspondence
Chemist/Manager
Louisville, KY 40205

DARWIN ON TRIAL

by Phillip E. Johnson
Regnery Gateway
Washington, DC (1991)

"Evolution" and "creation" can be defined in a number of different ways, Phillip Johnson points out, and they are not inevitably conflicting concepts; but "Darwinism" and Darwin stand for *fully naturalistic* evolution which excludes direction, purpose, intelligent creation or design. The scientific establishment claims Darwinism to be proven fact and it is wrong about that, says Johnson; nothing known to science disproves "creationism," the belief that life was created and its development guided by a Creator. (Johnson distinguishes this "creationism" from "creation-science," the fundamentalist claim of a six-day creation about 10,000 years ago, for which he maintains no brief.)

A different book could make the case soundly. No scientific theory is ever finally proven true (even while some scientists declare it to be so); it always remains just the best so-far-conceived way of connecting together certain known phenomena (even while that connecting together is called "making sense of" or "explaining"). Beliefs about God, morals, purpose, and ultimate origins are always immune to disproof by science, albeit such beliefs may seem more or less plausible in the light of scientific knowledge. Thus it seems to most of us nowadays quite implausible that the universe was created ten thousand years ago with every appearance of having evolved for about ten billion years; but implausible, even highly or absurdly implausible, does not validly convert into "impossible": by definition, human beings cannot know or understand the mind of God. Quite plausibly, it seems to many people, the laws of Nature under whose guidance the universe has developed were somehow chosen or established or initiated by an Intelligence. That plausibility and the former implausibility do not exhaust the possible reconciliations between what science now seems to know and what religion seems to have revealed.

But Phillip Johnson has chosen not to make this sound case; instead, he attacks Darwinism *within science*, and thereby misleads about science and about what science says about evolution. The widespread ignorance over these matters is illustrated by the reviewers who applauded this book, calling it for instance a "cogent, succinct inquiry [that] cuts like a knife through neo-Darwinist assumptions" (1). *National Review* (2) likes it because "you aren't likely to see it reviewed in the *Washington Post* or *The New York Review of Books*." *Christianity Today* (3) sees it as "a credible challenge to evolution's sweeping claims." On the other hand, the book was diagnosed in *Booklist* as "superficially logical and reasonable" (4); and David Hull in *Nature* (5) destroyed the book's pretensions with quiet but decisive authority. Reviews so polarized signal that ideologies are clashing.

In Chapter 5, "The Fact of Evolution," Johnson has a field day with the views of some of those — Isaac Asimov, John Dewey, Theodosius Dobzhansky, Julian Huxley, William Provine, Carl Sagan — who have dogmatically asserted that science demands atheism and a belief in purposeless evolution. Excessive claims by these gurus of science easily backfire; creationists are aided by them just as Velikovsky and his supporters were helped by the sloppy dogmatism of his critics (6). Johnson's case is assisted when he can quote Dobzhansky to the effect that "Evolution ... may conceivably be controlled by man"; Julian Huxley asserting that there is "no longer ... need or room for the supernatural ... [in view of] the evolutionary vision ... the new religion that we can be sure will arise"; and a president of the American Association for the Advancement of Science as saying "to doubt evolution is to doubt science, and science is only another name for truth." Stephen Jay Gould contends that "human beings evolved from ape-like ancestors," and Johnson corrects him: what we observe is similarity, not ancestry; "Gould draws the line between fact and theory in the wrong place" (pp. 66-7). One might add that Gould does so in a needlessly provocative way; he could with equal validity have said, "humans and apes have a common ancestry," or "apes evolved from human-like ancestors."

But Johnson himself is as prone as those he criticizes to the delusion that the paradigms of science are true: "[to] say that naturalistic evolution is *science* ... [is] not very different from saying ... true" (p.7); "unquestionably ... impressive explanatory power, but how are we to tell if it is *true*?" (p.66); "before we would be justified in concluding that Darwinism is probably true" (p. 89). Johnson asserts that the National Academy of Science "defined 'science' in such a way that advocates of supernatural creation may neither argue for their own position not dispute the claims of the scientific establishment" (p. 8). Not at all. No one is obliged to believe the conclusions that atheists draw from their interpretation of what science knows about evolution, just as no one is obliged to believe the conclusions that theistic evolutionists draw from the same body of scientific knowledge; it is just that outsiders to science should refrain from telling insiders how to do their job — just as Johnson and his colleagues would resist scientists telling them how the legal profession should go about its business.

Johnson does not understand that the conclusions of science are restricted to its own sphere of competence. Within that they are tentative even while research proceeds on the assumption that the current paradigms are true. Such belief is heuristic, not an article of faith. By supposing their beliefs to be true, scientists test them. If the assumption is wrong, Nature will sooner or later make that plain by producing inexplicable phenomena; then a scientific revolution follows and a new paradigm is established. Without a paradigm, there can be no organized research; and therefore a paradigm is never abandoned until a better alternative is available, no matter how unsatisfactory some of the paradigm's corollaries may have become. Though Johnson cites Kuhn to this effect (p. 120), he fails to understand it and writes as though there were something reprehensible about it: "However wrong the current answer ... it stands until a better ... arrives. It is as if a criminal defendant were not allowed to present an alibi unless he could also show who did commit the crime" (p. 8; see also pp. 28, 63, 154).

When Johnson says (p. 42), "supposing and believing are not enough to make a scientific explanation," he further reveals a lack of understanding; supposing and believing is precisely what goes on all the time, as tentative explanations are adduced at the frontiers of research. Johnson maintains that scientists "need more than ingenious excuses" (p. 54), but as the philosopher of science Imre Lakatos pointed out, the invention of ingenious excuses is precisely what scientists do to maintain the utility of the prevailing paradigm as long as possible.

Johnson thinks in terms of "the scientific method of inquiry, as articulated by Popper" (p. 154) — apparently unaware that Popper has few if any followers left. "Karl Popper provides the indispensable starting point for understanding the difference between science and pseudo-science" (p. 145) — not according to most philosophers of science, he doesn't, nor to those who have studied specific instances of so-called pseudo-science. "If Darwinists wanted to adopt Popper's standards for scientific inquiry ..." (p. 152) — but there are no mainstream scientists anywhere who want to do that.

"Access to the relevant scientific information presents no great difficulty," Johnson claims (p. 13). To the contrary, John Ziman has pointed out that although the scientific literature is open and publicly available, only experts can interpret it correctly. Johnson's book shows that he has read a lot of the right stuff, and he proves Ziman right because that reading has left him with quite mistaken views; for example, having explained pleiotropy and group selection, Johnson reveals that he doesn't understand their import (pp. 30-31). He could scarcely write "all frog species look pretty much alike ... but their molecules differ as much as those of mammals" (p. 90) if he understood how important it is to specify *which* molecules he means: DNA, hemoglobin, ATP, or what? And one who knows what mitochondria are must be taken aback to read that "mitochondrial DNA ... is passed only ... from mother to daughter" (p. 97), as though males had none. Here again there is a similarity with Immanuel Velikovsky and his ilk, the outsiders who think they can, by reading the literature, come to understand science well enough to engage in technical arguments with the insiders. It just isn't so. And like Velikovsky, Johnson cites unpublished and privately printed work (of Bowden, p. 175; of Thaxton, p. 183), thereby revealing his ignorance that a goodly part of the reliability of science stems from ignoring what has not passed the gauntlet of referees and editors. On prebiological evolution, he "particularly" recommends (p. 182) not only the excellent books by Cairns-Smith and by Robert Shapiro but also *The Mystery of Life's Origin* (by Charles Thaxton, Walter Bradley, and Roger Olsen) which displays the misunderstanding of thermodynamics typical of the creation-science Johnson claims to disavow.

In this book, as in the Velikovsky affair, there is much more rhetoric than substance. Labelling natural selection tautological (passim) is rhetorically powerful; but if one recalls that the environment has changed dramatically over the 4 to 5 billion years of the Earth's existence, by both slow "uniformitarian" change and periodic "catastrophism," it follows that quite different chance variations will have been selected for at different times (as well as in different places), so that the concept of such selection does make it plausible that an evolutionary pattern could emerge. To call "saltationist evolution" a "meaningless middle ground somewhere between evolution and special creation" (p. 61) is just an unfounded assertion that there is no point in looking for possible mechanisms of generic differentiation; to recall that Darwin thought it "rubbish" is beside the point since no living biologist feels obliged to agree with something just because Darwin said it. That a dissected coelacanth showed no amphibian traits tells us nothing at all about its presumed relatives of several hundred million years ago, never mind that Johnson takes it to suggest "that a rhipidistian fish might be equally disappointing to Darwinists if its soft body parts could be examined" (pp. 74-5); it might, yes, but equally it might not. "That 130 years of very determined efforts ... have done no better than ... a few ambiguous supporting examples" is for Johnson "significant negative evidence" (p. 84) when it is nothing of the sort; science progresses at its own pace, one thing after another; Johnson fails to acknowledge that biochemistry and molecular biology have discovered a host of similarities and relationships among all living things that were not known in Darwin's time. Scientists "never find evidence that contradicts the common ancestry thesis" not "because to Darwinists such evidence cannot exist" (p. 152) but simply because the evidence hasn't yet shown up: there are no human footprints dating from dinosaurian eras, nor are there fossil mammals from the pre-Cambrian era, to give only two out of a myriad of possible finds that would be incompatible with the concept of common ancestry and descent with modification.

Evidence that Johnson cannot deny he talks aside. The mammal-like reptiles, which show progressive change from reptile-like in the lower strata to mammal-like later, are dismissed because "the notion that mammals-in-general evolved from reptiles-in-general through a broad clump of therapsid lines is not Darwinism" (p. 76); maybe not, but it *is* consistent with the idea of evolution gradually under natural selection, which is the whole point, after all. "Darwinian transformation requires a single line of ancestral descent" (p. 76) only because this is the straw man that Johnson feels able to attack. The therapsids show that "for this example some sort of evolutionary model is preferable to the creation-science model of Gish, but ... does not qualify, or purport to qualify, as a genuine testing of the common ancestry hypothesis itself" (p. 174) only because Johnson says so; others would view the evolutionary hypothesis confirmed by the finding of this group not only intermediate between reptiles and mammals but even showing change from more like the one to more like the other.

Archaeopteryx cannot be explained away either, so Johnson calls it "a point for the Darwinists, but how important ...?"; "a possible bird ancestor rather than a certain one" (p. 79) — as though science were suggesting anything else. That there is "plenty of difficulty in imagining ... descendants as varied as the penguin, the humming bird, and the ostrich," no one denies, though scientists find it a challenge rather than an invitation to stop working at it or to deny the value of the evolutionary paradigm.

The subtlety of Johnson's rhetoric may be recognized best if one suggests paraphrases: for "scientific orthodoxy" (p. 3), read "currently most common scientific opinion"; chemical evolution did not achieve its "greatest" (p. 102) success in Miller's work of the 1950s, though one might legitimately call it the *earliest* success. Instead of saying evolution by macromutation is "impossible" (p. 37), say more correctly "not currently explicable or conceivable"; it is not that "to Darwinists unsolvable problems are not important" (p. 85), it is that scientists do not call problems *not yet solved* "unsolvable." For Darwinists "cannot demonstrate," for their "inability" (p. 142), read "cannot *yet* demonstrate" and "*present* inability." Calling "impossible to understand" what is merely not yet understood is a common ploy in these sorts of arguments. Also common is the citation of authorities as though they agreed with the author's main point when actually they do not; Johnson misleads in this fashion with De Beer (p. 172), Dose (p. 183), Eldredge (p. 60), Grene (pp. 171, 186), Kimura (p. 180), Mayr (p. 89), Raup (p. 171), and Shapiro (p. 183).

Johnson lumps all evolutionists together as Darwinists (pp. 4, 5, 9) to whom "the possibility that beyond the natural world there is a further reality which transcends science ... is absolutely unacceptable" (p. 110; see also pp. 8,101,114,127). Johnson doesn't understand that even Darwin's original "theory" contains at least five separate concepts that can be held independently. He doesn't understand the diversity that obtains within the scientific community, the republican working of that community in which there coexist umpteen different flavors of "evolutionist," when he confuses Judge Overton's finding that the conclusions of science are always tentative with the fact that (according to Johnson) "scientists are not in the least 'tentative'" (p. 113); that some scientists are dogmatic is no more to the point about what science has to say about evolution than the fact that some lawyers are dishonest tells us anything about the law's attitude toward honesty.

Johnson reveals the dogmatism of his own beliefs when he cites "the profound *dis*similarities between humans and animals of any kind" (p. 91) and says that "the positive evidence ... [for] Darwinian evolution ... is nonexistent" (p. 115); and he can be rather nasty about those he sees as his opponents: "the experts, meaning those who had the most to lose" (p. 82); "Richard Lewontin and Stephen Jay Gould have proudly claimed Marxist inspiration for their biological theories" (p. 135); "human descent from apes is not merely a scientific hypothesis; it is the secular equivalent of the story of Adam and Eve ... [which] requires a priesthood, in the form of thousands of researchers, teachers, and artists" (p. 83).

Why did Johnson feel the need to dispute Darwinist theory on its own ground, in the details where he cannot win, instead of on the broad and sound ground that science cannot disprove a wide range of possible religious beliefs? Because, it turns out, Johnson wishes a "supernatural Creator [who] not only initiated ... but in some meaningful sense *controls* ... [evolution] in furtherance of a purpose" (p. 4); and if one wants a Creator who intervenes tangibly, then one requires tangible evidence of intervention and is pushed to look for such evidence in "impossible" saltationist leaps between genera or classes or orders; one asserts that "in a word (Darwin's word), a saltation is equivalent to a miracle" (p. 32). Phillip Johnson "is creating something new" with this critique, according to *Christianity Today* (3). Not at all. Another lawyer made much the same argument twenty years ago (7), complete with the same misunderstandings of how science works and a reliance on Karl Popper for defining what science ought to be. New might be a discourse on the wide range of religious belief that remains plausible in the light of what science has learned about the physical mechanisms of life.

References

1. **Publishers Weekly**, 26 April 1991:51.

2. Doug Bandow, "Fossils and Fallacies," **National Review**, 29 April 1991:47-8.

3. Thomas Woodward, "A Professor Takes Darwin to Court," **Christianity Today**, 19 August 1991:33-5.

4. Stuart Whitwell, **Booklist**, 15 June 1991:1917.

5. David L. Hull, "The God of the Galapagos," **Nature**, 352(8 August 1991):485-6.

6. Henry H. Bauer (1984), **Beyond Velikovsky: The History of a Public Controversy**, Urbana & Chicago: University of Illinois Press. Especially Chapter 13, "Blundering Critics."

7. Norman Macbeth (1971), **Darwin Retried: An Appeal to Reason**, Boston: Gambit.

This review was originally published in the *Journal of Scientific Exploration* 6(2), and is reprinted by permission.

Henry H. Bauer
Professor of Chemistry and Science Studies
Virginia Polytechnic Institute and State University
Blacksburg, VA 24061

DARWIN ON TRIAL

by Phillip E. Johnson
Regnery Gateway
Washington, DC (1991)

I teach a course at Harvard with philosopher Robert Nozick and lawyer Alan Dershowitz. We take major issues engaged by each of our professions — from abortion to racism to right-to-die — and we try to explore and integrate our various approaches. We raise many questions and reach no solutions.

Clearly, I believe in this interdisciplinary exercise, and I accept the enlightenment that intelligent outsiders can bring to the puzzles of a discipline. The differences in approach are so fascinating — and each valid in its own realm. Philosophers will dissect the logic of an argument, an exercise devoid of empirical content, well past the point of glaze over scientific eyes (and here I blame scientists for their parochiality, for all the world's empirics cannot save an argument falsely formulated). Lawyers face a still different problem that makes their enterprise even more divergent from science — and for two major reasons.

First, the law must reach a decision even when insufficient evidence exists for confident judgement. (Scientists often err in the opposite direction of overcaution, even when the evidence is compelling, if not watertight.) Thus, in capital cases, the law must free a probably guilty man whose malfeasance cannot be proved beyond a doubt (a moral principle that seems admirable to me but would not work well in science). We operate with probabilities; the law must often traffic in absolutes.

Second, there is no "natural law" waiting to be discovered "out there" (*pace* Clarence Thomas in his recent testimony). Legal systems are human inventions, based on a history of human thought and practice. Consequently, the law gives decisive weight to the history of its own development — hence the rule of precedent in deciding cases. Scientists work in an opposite way: we search continually for new signals from nature to invalidate a history of past argument. (As a sometime historian of science, I wish that scientists, like lawyers, would pay more attention to, and have more reverence for, their pasts — but I understand why this is not likely to happen.)

Phillip E. Johnson is a law professor at Berkeley and "a philosophical theist and a Christian" who strongly believes in "a Creator who plays an active role in worldly affairs." His book has received great "play" in print and television, largely (I suppose) because such unconventional products rarely emanate from the symbolic home of California "flowerpower." The press loves an oddity. This publicity is certainly no measure of the book's merit, as I shall argue. Now, I most emphatically do not claim that a lawyer shouldn't poke his nose into our domain; nor do I hold that an attorney couldn't write a good book about evolution. A law professor might well compose a classic about the rhetoric and style of evolutionary discourse; subtlety of argument, after all, is a lawyer's business. But, to be useful in this way, a lawyer would have to understand and use our norms and rules, or at least tell us where we err in our procedures; he cannot simply trot out some applicable criteria from his own world and falsely condemn us from a mixture of ignorance and inappropriateness. Johnson, unfortunately, has taken the low road in writing a very bad book entitled *Darwin on Trial*.

In a "classic" of antievolutionary literature from the generation just past, lawyer Norman Macbeth (1971) wrote a much better book from the same standpoint, entitled *Darwin Retried* (titles are not subject to copyright). Macbeth ultimately failed (though he raised some disturbing points along the way) because he used an inappropriate legal criterion: the defendant (an opponent of evolution) is accused by the scientific establishment and must be acquitted if the faintest shadow of doubt can be raised against Darwinism. (As science is not a discipline that claims to establish certainty, all its conclusions would fall by this inappropriate procedure.)

Johnson's current incarnation of this false strategy, *Darwin on Trial*, hardly deserves to be called a book at all. It is, at best, a long magazine article promoted to hard covers — a clumsy, repetitious abstract argument with no weighing of evidence, no careful reading of literature on all sides, no full citation of sources (the book does not even contain a bibliography) and occasional use of scientific literature only to score rhetorical points. I see no evidence that Johnson has ever visited a scientist's laboratory, has any concept of quotidian work in the field or has read widely beyond writing for nonspecialists and the most "newsworthy" of professional claims.

The book, in short, is full of errors, badly argued, based on false criteria, and abysmally written. Didn't anyone ever teach Johnson not to end chapters with "announcement sentences" or to begin subsequent sections with summaries? Chapter 6, for example, ends with a real zinger: "We will look at that claim in the next chapter." The very next chapter then begins with the maximally lively: "Before we try to get any answers out of the molecular evidence, we had better review where we stand." Mrs. McInerney, my tough but beloved third-grade teacher, would have rapped his knuckles sore for such a construction, used by Johnson at almost every chapter transition.

Johnson is not a "scientific creationist" of Duane Gish's ilk — the "young earth" Biblical literalists who have caused so much political trouble of late, but whom we beat in the Supreme Court in 1987. He accepts the earth's great age and allows that God may have chosen to work via natural selection and other evolutionary principles (though He may also operate by miraculous intervention if and when He chooses). Johnson encapsulates his major insistence by writing: "In the broadest sense, a 'creationist' is simply a person who believes that the world (and especially mankind) was *designed*, and exists for a *purpose*." Darwinism, Johnson claims, inherently and explicitly denies such a belief and therefore constitutes a naturalistic philosophy intrinsically opposed to religion.

But this is the oldest canard and non sequitur in the debater's book. To say it for all my colleagues and for the umpteenth millionth time (from college bull sessions to learned treatises): science simply cannot (by its legitimate methods) adjudicate the issue of God's possible superintendence of nature. We neither affirm nor deny it; we simply can't comment on it as scientists. If some of our crowd have made untoward statements claiming that Darwinism disproves God, then I will find Mrs. McInerney and have their knuckles rapped for it (as long as she can equally treat those members of our crowd who have argued that Darwinism must be God's method of action). Science can work only with naturalistic explanations; it can neither affirm nor deny other types of actors (like God) in other spheres (the moral realm, for example).

Forget philosophy for a moment; the simple empirics of the past hundred years should suffice. Darwin himself was agnostic (having lost his religious beliefs upon the tragic death of his favorite daughter), but the great American botanist Asa Gray, who favored natural selection and wrote a book entitled *Darwiniana*, was a devout Christian. Move forward 50 years: Charles D. Walcott, discoverer of the Burgess Shale fossils, was a convinced Darwinian and an equally firm Christian, who believed that God had ordained natural selection to construct a history of life according to His plans and purposes. Move on another 50 years to the two greatest evolutionists of our generation: G.G. Simpson was a humanistic agnostic, Theodosius Dobzhansky a believing Russian Orthodox. Either half my colleagues are enormously stupid, or else the science of Darwinism is fully compatible with conventional religious beliefs — and equally compatible with atheism, thus proving that the two great realms of nature's factuality and the source of human morality do not strongly overlap.

But Johnson's major premise — the inherent Godlessness of Darwinism — could be wrong, and he might still have a good argument for the major thrust of his text: the attempt to show that Darwinism is a dogma, unsupported by substantial and meaningful evidence, and propped up by false logic. But here he fails utterly, almost comically (Macbeth's 1971 book is much better).

Johnson's line of argument collapses in two major ways, the second more serious than the first. I feel a bit more forgiveness in this first category — familiarity with the facts of biology — because the field is immense and alien to Johnson's training. Still, the density of simple error is so high that I must question wider competence when attempts at extension yield such poor results. To cite just a few examples from the compendium of Johnson's factual and terminological errors: On page 16, he claims that all immediate variation for natural selection comes from mutation: "Darwinian evolution postulates two elements. The first is what Darwin called 'variation,' and what scientists today call *mutation*." He then realizes that he has neglected sexual recombination, the vastly predominant source of immediate variation in sexual species, but he makes his error worse by including recombination as a category of mutation. On page 30, he reports that "sexual selection is a relatively minor component in Darwinist theory today." But sexual selection is perhaps the hottest Darwinian topic of the past decade, subject of at least a dozen books (which Johnson has neither noted nor read — a sure sign of his unfamiliarity with current thinking in evolutionary theory). On page 41, he states that polyploidy (as a result of doubling of chromosomes) can occur only in "hermaphrodite species capable of self-fertilization" — and therefore can play little role in major change (for self-doubling does not yield markedly new qualities). But the evolutionarily potent form of polyploidy is not the autoploidy that he equates with the entire phenomenon, but alloploidy, or doubling of both male and female components after fertilization with pollen of a different species.

On page 60, he calls the German paleontologist Otto Schindewolf a saltationist, whereas Schindewolf's subtle theory contained a central element of insensible change in a process that he called proterogenesis (gradual seepage of juvenile traits into adult stages). Schindewolf spent most of his career studying small and continuous changes in ammonite suture patterns. On page 103, Johnson raises the old chestnut against a natural origin of earthly life by arguing: "the possibility that such a complex entity could assemble itself by chance is fantastically unlikely." Sure, and no scientist has used that argument for 20 years, now that we understand so much more about the self-organizing properties of molecules and other physical systems. The list goes on.

Second, and more important for documenting Johnson's inadequacy in his own realm of expertise, he performs abysmally in the lawyer's domain of the art of argument. To begin, he simply does not grasp (or chooses not to understand) the purpose and logic of evolutionary argument. I have already illustrated his central conflation of Darwinism with hostility to religion. I was particularly offended by his false and unkind accusation that scientists are being dishonest when they claim equal respect for science and religion: "Scientific naturalists do not see a contradiction, because they never meant that the realms of science and religion are of equal dignity and importance. Science for them is the realm of objective knowledge; religion is a matter of subjective belief. The two should not conflict because a rational person always prefers objective knowledge to subjective belief." Speak for yourself, Attorney Johnson. I regard the two as of equal dignity and limited contact. "The two should not conflict," because science treats factual reality, while religion struggles with human morality. I do not view moral argument as a whit less important than factual investigation.

Johnson then upholds the narrow and blinkered caricature of science as experiment and immediate observation only. Doesn't he realize that all historical science, not just evolution, would disappear by his silly restriction? Darwin, he writes, "described *The Origin of Species* as 'one long argument,' and the point of the argument was that the common ancestry thesis was so logically appealing that rigorous empirical testing was not required. He proposed no daring experimental tests, and thereby started his science on the wrong road." But Darwin spent 20 years collecting facts for evolution. The *Origin* is one long compendium of observations and empirical confirmations. To be sure, Darwin's method is not generally experimental, for singular and complex past events are not so explained by any historical science. Darwin thought long and hard about proper methodology of confirmation for historical science and used Whewell's "consilience of induction," or bringing of widely disparate information under a uniquely consistent explanation. Darwin wrote of his method in 1868: "This hypothesis may be tested ... by trying whether it explains several large and independent classes of facts; such as the geological succession of organic beings, their distribution in past and present times, and their mutual affinities and homologies."

Not only does Johnson misconstrue the basic principles of our science (as I have shown), but he also fails to present cogent arguments in his own brief as well. His development of a case is fatally marred by three pervasive techniques of careless or unfair discourse.

First, omissions that unjustly castigate a person or a claim. On page 5, Johnson recounts the tale of H.F. Osborn and his error in identifying a pig tooth as a human ancestor: "Osborn prominently featured 'Nebraska Man' ... in his antifundamentalist newspaper articles and radio broadcasts, until the tooth was discovered to be from a peccary." True, but who made the correction? Although Johnson does not tell us, the answer is H.F. Osborn, who properly tested his claim by mounting further collecting expeditions, discovering his error and correcting it — in other words, science working at its best.

On page 74, in his lick-and-promise tour through the history of vertebrates, we learn that no intermediary has ever been discovered between rhipidistian fishes and early amphibians. Yet Johnson never mentions the first amphibians, *Ichthyostega* and *Acanthostega* (featured in all paleontological texts) with their conserved features of a fishy past: small tail fins, lateral line systems, and six to eight digits on each limb. On page 76, he admits my own claim for intermediacy in the defining anatomical transition between reptiles and mammals: passage of the reptilian jaw-joint bones into the mammalian middle ear. Trying to turn clear defeat to advantage, he writes: "We may concede Gould's narrow point." Narrow indeed; what more does he want? Then we find out: "On the other hand, there are many important features by which mammals differ from reptiles besides the jaw and ear bones, including the all-important reproductive systems." Now how am I supposed to uncover fossil evidence of hair, lactation and live birth? A profession finds the very best evidence it could, in exactly the predicted form and time, and a lawyer still tries to impeach us by rhetorical trickery. No wonder lawyer jokes are so popular in our culture.

Second, consider Johnson's false use of synecdoche. The art of having an item or part stand for the whole is a noble trope in poetry and *the* classical, unfair trick of debate. Professions are big, and everyone makes a stupid statement now and again. As an honorable opponent, you cannot use a single dumb argument to characterize an entire field. Yet Johnson does so again and again — and this, I suppose, represents the legal tactic of "poke any hole and win acquittal." Thus, Johnson quotes a few ill-informed statements, representing opposite extremes around a golden mean held by nearly every evolutionist — that natural selection is either meaningless as tautology or necessarily and encompassingly true as an a priori universal principle. Now both claims have been advanced, but they are held by tiny minorities and unsustained by any strong or enduring argument. The principle of natural selection does not collapse because a few individuals fall into fallacies from opposite sides of claiming too little or too much. Similarly, the consensus that science and religion are separate and equally valuable is not brought down by the fact that Julian Huxley unites them on one side, while Will Provine holds that science implies atheism on the other. Minorities are not necessarily wrong (or science would never advance), but only the cogency of their data and arguments, not the mere fact of their existence, brings down old theories.

As his third trick, Johnson continues to castigate evolutionists for old and acknowledged errors. T.H. Huxley, paraphrasing Dryden's famous line about Alexander the Great's drunken boasting, stated that life is too short to occupy oneself with the slaying of the slain more than once. In law, the illogicality of an important precedent might bring down a current structure like a house of cards. But in science, a bad old argument is just a superfluous fossil. Nothing is gained by exposing a 30-year-old error — save the obvious point that science improves by correcting its past mistakes. Yet Johnson continually tilts at such rotted windmills. He attacks Simpson's data from the 1950s on mammalian polyphyly (while we have accepted the data of mammalian monophyly for at least 15 years). He quotes Ernst Mayr from 1963, denying neutrality of genes in principle. But much has changed in 30 years, and Mayr is as active as ever at age 87. Why not ask him what he thinks now?

Johnson's grandiose claims, backed by such poor support in fact and argument, recall a variety of phrases from a mutually favorite source: "He that troubleth his own house shall inherit the wind" (Proverbs 11:29, and source for the famous play that dramatized the Scopes trial); "They have sown the wind, and they shall reap the whirlwind" (Hosea 8:7). But *Darwin on Trial* just isn't good enough to merit such worrisome retorts. The book is scarcely more than an acrid little puff — and I therefore close with a famous line from Darwin's soulmate, born on the same day of February 12, 1809. Abraham Lincoln wrote: "'And this, too, shall pass away.' How much it expresses! How chastening in the hour of pride! How consoling in the depths of affliction!"

This review was originally published as "Impeaching a Self-Appointed Judge" in *Scientific American* 267(1) in July 1992, and is reprinted by permission.

Stephen Jay Gould
Museum of Comparative Zoology
Harvard University
Cambridge, MA 02138

HANDY DANDY EVOLUTION REFUTER

by Robert E.Kofahl
Beta Books
San Diego, CA (1980)

The real purpose of this book is stated in an appendix which concludes:

The *Handy Dandy Evolution Refuter* provides logic and scientific evidence to show that materialistic evolutionary theories are really not science, and that there is actually no scientifically based reason for ignoring or refusing the gracious offer of God to save those who believe in His Son Jesus Christ. It is our hope that our readers will come to faith, or to stronger faith in the Bible and in the God of the Bible Who is Creator, Lord, and Judge of the world.

This conclusion is not the only religious statement to be found in the book. The authors have a two-fold purpose: to deprecate the concept of evolution as a network of valid scientific theories, and to offer evidence for a putatively literal interpretation of the biblical account of creation.

The *Refuter* is organized in what many will recognize as a catechism format. Each section is a sequence of questions or statements that are highlighted in bold print, each such question or statement followed by a brief discussion or answer. The book is therefore a kind of guide to responding concisely and critically to almost every aspect of evolutionary theory. The topics treated cover the broad range typical of "creation science" books. One by one, each topic, from the limitations of science to estimates of the age of the earth, is redefined and distorted in such a way as to make the evolutionary explanation look foolish, or to offer divine creation as an equally likely explanation.

The limits of science are redefined so that only observable, repeatable, and experimentally verifiable phenomena can be valid scientific subjects. Thus, since no one witnessed the origin of the universe or of life, theories of their origin are matters of faith. Furthermore, even should a scientist be able to form a living organism from nonliving materials, this success would actually confirm the validity of creationism, since the experiment would have required an intelligent designer — the basic assertion of the "creation model" concerning the origin of life. In reality, the sole limitation of the scientific process is that it can only deal with questions relating to the material universe. Thus, any process which invokes the intervention of supernatural forces is outside the realm of science. Science can deal with historical events as long as hypotheses are constructed with reference to observable natural processes. Any attempt to develop a living system in a laboratory will have to be done within the constraints of what we know about conditions on the early Earth.

The book is essentially a listing of the common "scientific creationist" attacks on evolutionary theory. The spontaneous origin of life is shown by probability theory to be "impossible," using the faulty analogy of flipping a coin and having it come up heads a large number of times. The coin flipping analogy ignores the fact that evolution works in an incremental fashion based on some existing, working system. A cell did not randomly form out of a "soup" of organic molecules. Rather, early self-replicating systems evolved more and more of the features of cells by the same processes of mutation and selection as operate today. Evolution, which is incorrectly described as implying an inevitable increase in order and complexity, is said to violate the Second Law of Thermodynamics, which is here renamed the Natural Law of Degeneration. However, the Second Law of Thermodynamics applies to closed systems without any outside energy sources, and all living systems depend on outside energy sources. Furthermore, evolution does not predict increasing levels of complexity. For example, natural selection is a very opportunistic process which is limited by available genetic variation and the interactions among organisms and the current environment. Mammals are not "better" or more "complex" than reptiles, but the combination of selection and unique historical events has resulted in an explosive radiation of mammals over the last 65 million years. The fossil record is said to be devoid of transitional forms, and such examples as ancestral horses and *Archaeopteryx* are dismissed as being the result of the atheistic philosophical biases of evolutionary biologists.

Physics, astronomy, and oceanography are not spared criticism, because these fields have also been permeated by evolutionary philosophy. All forms of radioactive dating are disposed of as being based on questionable or unproven assumptions. Kofahl cites several references (almost all from "creation science" sources) which indicate that an unbiased understanding of astrophysics would lead to the conclusion that the solar system and the universe are only several thousand years old. Similarly, the salinity of the ocean, the depth of its sediments, and even the mass of the Mississippi delta are said to indicate that this planet is much younger than most scientists accept.

The truly interesting parts of the book are the sections in which the "creation model" is discussed in detail. For example, the biblical account of Eve's creation from Adam's rib is said to make sense in the light of modern genetics because, if it had been the other way around, with Adam made from Eve's rib, how could Adam have acquired a Y chromosome? The entire human species could easily have descended from Noah's family of 8 persons if each subsequent couple produced an average of 2.3 children. But in his discussion of inbreeding the author is self-contradictory: at one point he states that the intensive inbreeding that early population growth would have required was not detrimental because Adam, Eve, and Noah had not yet acquired the high genetic load of modern humans; elsewhere he speculates that some presumptive pre-human ancestors were actually full human beings who had degenerated due to inbreeding in isolated populations after the flood. Of course, not the slightest evidential basis is given for any of these wild pseudo-scientific speculations.

Many of the erroneous statements in this book are made to seem accurate by references to scientific literature, whether apt or not. Also, each major section ends with a few "quotable quotes." Abundant scientific quotation is a standard creationist ploy, and it is doubtful that many of the book's readers will bother to check sources. They would often find that quotations are inappropriate or have been lifted out of context.

A final point worth mentioning is Dr. Kofahl's implication in several places that evolutionary theory is supported by some vast conspiracy. Not only are scientists depicted as blinded by their evolutionary preconceptions, but also as having worked to ignore or suppress evidence in favor of creation. Cited as examples of such unseemly behavior are the Paluxy River tracks, which are claimed to show human and dinosaur footprints in the same strata; and the Castenedolo and Calaveras fossil specimens, which are described as in the "wrong place" to demonstrate human evolution. However, several studies have shown that, if there is any fraud or bias involved in the Paluxy River tracks, it rests with those who have used them to support "creation science." In the other cases, the Castenedolo remains were shown to have been the result of deliberate burial in older geological material, and the Calaveras skull was recognized as a hoax soon after its discovery. In both cases, these conclusions are based on published documentation, but the author was either unaware of or chose to ignore the information. Piltdown Man is cited as an evolutionary fraud, but it is not mentioned that evolution-oriented paleontologists uncovered the fraud. Perhaps the most interesting claim in the book is the dismissal of the Scopes Trial with the statement that "the ACLU, long noted for its defense of left-wing causes, perpetrated a fraud on the court and on the public" because Scopes never actually taught the lesson on evolution with which he was charged. The last statement is probably true; was the lawsuit then a fraud?

In summation, this book is devoid of any scientific or pedagogical value. Its intent is primarily religious, and its approach is to restructure scientific knowledge in order to fit a particular religious tradition. Its sole useful function — and here its value no doubt is great — is to serve as a handy-dandy sourcebook for creationist debaters and special pleaders.

Erik P. Scully
Biology Department
Towson State University
Towson, MD 21204

THE NATURAL LIMITS TO BIOLOGICAL CHANGE

Lane P. Lester and Raymond G. Bohlin
Zondervan Publishing House
Grand Rapids, MI
Probe Ministries International
Dallas, TX (1984)

The last section of the last chapter of this book is titled, "The Controversy: A Call to Reason." The authors attribute emotionalism on the creation/evolution controversy to "a lack of understanding of the basic presuppositions of the two polarized positions" and to the fact that "the question of origins deals with history — i.e. unique events."

Citing Karl Popper (1980), the authors say that "evolution in the broad sense, from molecules to man, is not directly testable ... [but that] one can *derive* predictions that in *many* cases can be tested." They make the same claim for their own creationist theory, that "there may be definable limits to biological change." Neither side, they say, is likely to reject its "complete metaphysical package" on the basis of a single falsified hypothesis; rather, other adjustments will be made. Such flexibility allows "theorists from both sides ... to explain essentially all the relevant data within the confines of their own model."

The authors quote physicist David Bohm and philosopher of science John C. Greene on the hazards of failing to recognize the presuppositions of one's worldview. They cite S. J. Gould on the "cultural and political biases" that allegedly influenced Darwin's gradualism, and Michael Ruse on those that allegedly influenced Gould's concept of punctuated equilibrium, and they suggest that creationists are just as entitled to have their biases. "Objective evidence is available in support of Neo-Darwinism, punctuated equilibria, and creation. Each individual must weigh and interpret the evidence through his own world view and decide which fits reality most consistently. At present, all three are defended by educated individuals trained in a broad spectrum of science ... none can be shown to be totally implausible ... Truth is not arrived at by majority vote."

The creationist authors of this book certainly are "educated individuals." Lane Lester received a Ph.D. in genetics from Purdue University. For some years now he has been a professor of biology at Liberty Baptist College (renamed Liberty University in 1985). Raymond Bohlin received an M.S. in population genetics from North Texas State University and, as of the publication date of this book, was a doctoral student in molecular biology at the University of Texas, Dallas.

Chapters two and three of their book provide a generally accurate review of biological variation, examples of adaptation, the DNA-protein synthesis story, gene regulation, chromosomes, and mutation. Chapters four and six describe neo-Darwinism ("the synthetic theory") and punctuationalism, respectively. Chapters five and seven "dissect what the critics have labelled fallacious, exaggerated, or misunderstood" about the theory described in the previous chapter.

The authors say, "though no one can claim to be totally objective in such a discussion, our hope is that both sides will observe that they are fairly and adequately (though necessarily incompletely) represented." The authors succeed better in the two descriptive chapters that in the two critical ones, though I found all four to be useful to me personally. Nearly all the 155 citations in these four chapters are to respectable literature, presumably including a paper by Bohlin and Zimmerman (*J. Mammalogy* 63:218).

How their critique fails is illustrated by the following. Evolutionary theory obviously requires mutations that generate novel phenotypes. Lester and Bohlin (p.87) say that, at best, "A mutation in a structural gene will not produce anything new, just a minor variation of what already exists." But what if, as a result of the mutation, the catalytic powers of the protein product are substantially altered, leading to new chemical reactions?

The authors point out that studies on the evolution of hemoglobins claim no drastically new function. Similarly, "cytochrome c will remain cytochrome c," no matter how much it is changed by mutation — or it will lose its function entirely. "Possible exceptions," they say (p.92), "are two isolated examples of similar proteins that perform different functions": human insulin is similar to mouse nerve-growth factor, and alpha-lactalbumin is similar to tear-lysozyme. They suggest that these similarities may be due to underlying similarities in function and in place of origin. "With only these two examples," they say, "it is difficult to determine whether these two are similar proteins because of direct descent or not, though it remains a possibility." Even ignoring the fact that they have not done justice to the literature on similar proteins with distinct functions (as they imply they have), the examples they cite actually provide clues as to how mutation can lead to new functions.

Unlike some of their creationist colleagues, Lester and Bohlin (p. 84) admit that, in the self-critical literature of evolutionary science they cite, "evolution itself is not questioned, just its mechanism." In fact, the main point of chapters four through seven is to stress uncertainties about evolutionary mechanisms. Chapter seven concludes by objecting to the claim (made by S. J. Gould and others) that evolution is both fact and theory. ("The fact is that it occurred; the theory concerns how it occurred.") Lester and Bohlin cite Gould as asserting that continental drift wasn't accepted until plate tectonics provided a mechanism. They say (p. 148) "Evolution is supposed to be a fact, yet like continental drift earlier, it consists mainly of circumstantial evidence, with no documented mechanism. One gets the feeling that a double standard is in operation."

In fact, there are striking parallels between acceptance of biological evolution by the scientific community after 1859 and its acceptance of continental drift 100 years later. Both concepts were seriously advocated half a century before acceptance. Both won acceptance after much more evidence, of diverse kinds, was amassed. That evidence included plausible concepts that helped explain how the phenomenon could occur. Since acceptance, vastly more evidence has been amassed, and great strides have been made in describing the mechanisms involved. Significant questions remain unanswered. And in both cases the scientific community is confident that those questions can and will be answered, and that those answers will not jeopardize the main claims of the theory. Regarding the fundamental ideas that life evolved and that continents drift, today's scientific community does not exhibit the sense of unease that presages scientific revolutions.

Since Lester and Bohlin cannot bring themselves to share in today's scientific consensus, their last chapter (eight) offers "another alternative" to "the two major competing models of evolutionary change." They insist (p. 162), and I agree, that if their "theory of the created kind is to be rejected, let it be for lack of scientific integrity and not because its inspiration is biblical."

Their "alternative" is to postulate created kinds, which they call "prototypes." "In the broad sense, by a prototype we mean 'all organisms that are descended from a single created population'." (p. 162) (Maybe they avoided the pre-Darwinian term "archetype" because it was used in a way that would encompass many "prototypes," at a time when species were regarded as fixed.) A prototype may include only one species or "dozens" of species. It might even include several higher taxa, since such categories are subjectively assigned anyway. So evolution can occur within, but only within, prototypes.

Lester and Bohlin argue (p. 156-7) against previously offered creationist criteria for defining created kinds (Marsh's genetic fusion and Jones' cortomes). The constraints to change, they say, must be in the organisms' DNA, and more likely in its regulatory structure than in structural genes. (Much remains to be learned about regulatory mechanisms, and evolutionists, too, expect studies in this field to solve problems with their theory.)

To define the limits of prototypes, the authors say all the usual taxonomic criteria must be considered, but they believe (p. 165) "that all members of a prototype will possess the same regulatory and developmental pathways. Since the 'rules of grammar' do not originate by natural processes, the regulatory and developmental pathways will remain stable through speciation and mutation events. These pathways will differ from one prototype to the next." So, they argue, their model makes predictions and meets the criterion of testability. But they don't explain how they will interpret developmental pathways shared by a wide variety of organisms (all vertebrates, for example), or how they will distinguish pathways that define a prototype from those that don't, or how they will show that the prototype-defining pathways are immutable.

They expect (pp. 165-7) that regulatory differences between humans and the great apes will show them to be in different prototypes, even though "genic and highly detailed chromosome studies show an unexpectedly high degree of similarity." More than a page is devoted to explaining why these similarities aren't definitive. They don't mention the recent hybrid between a gibbon and a siamang, two species that differ much more in chromosomal composition than do humans and chimps (*Science* 205:308).

On page 172 they argue that "*Homo erectus* is fully human, but in a degenerate state." This idea, they say, shows the value of the creationist perspective because it leads to "research questions otherwise unasked." Similarly, the creationist hypothesis would generate research seeking functional significance for amino acid sequence differences between "homologous" proteins. They ignore the fact that "adaptationist" evolutionary biologists have long sought functional significance for every identifiable feature of organisms.

Literature cited in chapter eight varies widely in quality, and the section on "Creation" under "For Further Reading" lists four creationist books of low repute.

Well, what to make of all this?

I think Lester and Bohlin are sensitive to the criticisms that have been levelled against creationist argumentation, and they largely avoid the tricks for which the Institute for Creation Research is infamous.

Of course, Lester and Bohlin do not accept the principle that miracles have no place in scientific explanation. In fact, they argue that nature contains unmistakable evidence of intelligent design, notably the genetic code. They ignore naturalistic possibilities, such as those suggested by Eigen et al. (*Scientific American* 244(4):88) or Cairns-Smith (*Scientific American* 252(6):90). They also ignore critiques of the "argument from design," beginning with David Hume's classic *Dialogues Concerning Natural Religion* (1979). They ignore the fact that the "universal intent" of science dictates that science limit itself to naturalistic explanations. In fact, when I visited him in 1980, Lester told me that he doesn't divide the world into natural and supernatural: after all, whatever is, is. But the natural/supernatural dichotomy seeks to isolate those matters where there is reason to hope for universal agreement.

To creationists, universal acceptance of their beliefs is a distant dream. Their first priority is merely to establish them as *possible*. Establishing them as one *plausible* alternative among others would be even better. This is Lester and Bohlin's goal. I, for one, am willing to consider as "possible" any of the myriad scenarios that I can imagine. But for their creationist hypothesis to be plausible requires much more than gaps in the fossil record, limits on changes achieved in breeding programs, and biological complexity.

Lester and Bohlin discuss the possible radiation of the diverse Hawaiian honeycreepers from an original "prototype" population "in the estimated 5-million-year existence of the oldest Hawaiian island" (pp. 143-144). When, in 1980, Lester and I discussed the age of the earth, he was willing to give it longer than Henry Morris' maximum of 10,000 years. Lester thought it might be as old as 50,000. It may be that, like Liberty University's chancellor Falwell, he now allows for the possibility of greater age. But I suspect that Lester still insists on the accuracy of the Genesis account of Noah's flood. If so, did Noah live more than 5 million years ago? And how was the great store of genetic variability that allowed the honeycreepers to diversify transmitted through the two prototypical honeycreepers in the ark? Or was Noah's flood more recent, and was the ark overloaded with more than one pair representing each kind? It is possible that Lester, like Henry Morris, is no longer eager to discuss Noah's flood in a scientific context, on grounds that *nature* tells us nothing about Noah. But if Lester still insists that there was a world-wide flood, questions arise as to when it occurred, how animals and plants survived it, and how answers to these questions fit in with the concept of speciating prototypes.

If "creation scientists" want us to consider their theories, they should also be willing to flesh them out for us. They have a long way to go before they can match the comprehensive explanatory system of evolutionary theory — even though it, too, poses as yet unanswered questions. The validity of so many of the components of evolutionary theory has been demonstrated. Lester and Bohlin hope that the same can be done for the components of their explanatory system, but they do not adequately specify test criteria and they provide no evidence that nature will cooperate.

It is a truism that everyone has biases and ultimately decides for himself what makes sense to him. But would-be scholars are expected to labor mightily to overcome their biases. More than most others who call themselves "creation scientists," Lester and Bohlin give the appearance of having done this. But ultimately they resort to the truism to justify their special pleading.

This review was originally published as "Lane Lester's Limits" in the *Creation/Evolution Newsletter* 7(1), and is reprinted by permission.

Karl D. Fezer
Professor of Biology
Concord College
Athens, WV 24712

EVOLUTION AND THE MODERN CHRISTIAN

by Henry M. Morris
Baker Book House
Grand Rapids, MI (1967)

The stated intent of this book is to "open the minds and hearts of young people to the true Biblical cosmology." To accomplish this, the author requires the reader to accept without question Biblical revelation as actual recorded history. He fails to tell his reader that today many Christians accept that a number of different literary genres are used in the Bible. Through out the book, he links the theory of evolution to "Bad News" and delusions of Satan, while associating creation theory with the "Good News."

Science, including the First and Second Laws of Thermodynamics, is used and misused in attempts to discredit evolution and support creationism. However, by the end of Chapter 1, the author has already concluded that "the entire question of origins (whether by creation or evolution) is really outside the domain of science, not being susceptible to scientific experimentation and analysis. Knowledge of origins must come from outside of science – it is, therefore, not really a scientific question at all."

The reasons for trying to place the entire question of origin outside of science soon become apparent. The author accepts the Usher date of 4004 B.C. for creation. However, he would accept an upper limit of 10,000 to 15,000 years ago for creation of the Earth. Thus his three great events of history – Creation, the Fall, and the Flood – must have taken place within a maximum of 15,000 years. To accept these dates, he must ignore or discredit ever-growing lines of evidence from paleontology, stratigraphy, and radiocarbon dating that show the Earth is much older than 15,000 years.

The author would like science to be restricted to those areas where experiments or measurements can be performed at different times and the same results obtained. Since we do not know and cannot control the different factors involved in the origin of life or the universe, experimental reproducibility cannot be documented. Thus evolution cannot be documented using "true science," and according to Morris, evolution is a matter of faith and not science. Fortunately for those of us involved in earth science and related areas, not everyone accepts Morris's narrow view of science. He attempts to use science to confuse his readers so that both evolution and creation become matters of faith rather than of fact.

The scientific value of the book is nil; the author selectively chooses the areas of science that he accepts, and rejects other areas of generally accepted science (which he chooses to ignore, or attempts to discredit in a very biased manner). Science is systematized knowledge, and this is absent from Morris's book, where much accepted knowledge is outside the field of science and is a matter of faith. His book may be suitable for a philosophy or religion course, but should not be used in a public school science class.

T.E. Fenton
Professor of Agronomy
Iowa State University
Ames, IA 50011

SCIENTIFIC CREATIONISM

Public School Edition
by Henry M. Morris
Creation-Life Publishers
San Diego, CA (1974)

This book repeatedly claims "to treat the subject of origins with no references to the Bible or to religious doctrine. The treatment is positive, rather than negative, showing that the creation model of origins and history may be used to correlate the facts of science at least as effectively as the evolution model."

As a physics teacher, I taught the law of inertia to be the assertion, first made by Galileo, that "any velocity once imparted to a body will be rigidly maintained as long as there are no causes of acceleration or retardation, a condition which is approached only on horizontal planes where the force of friction has been minimized." *Scientific Creationism* makes a statement that contrasts with Galileo's nearly 400-year-old discovery. According to Morris, "... everywhere in space and time occur phenomena and processes. These manifest omnipresent energy perpetually generating motion.... This fact argues for an omnipotent Cause in such energies and motion, and also for a completed creation in the past, in accord with the creation model" (p. 21). Simply stated, the law of inertia has been replaced in the creation model with the law of an "omnipotent Cause," and creationists claim that this can be taught to students with no reference to religious doctrine.

The conservation of mass was a belief held by the Greeks as early as the fifth century B.C. James Joule laboriously worked out our modern concept of the conservation of energy more that 140 years ago. Quite a number of scientists contributed to the discovery of the laws of thermodynamics, and yet I was astounded to read (pp. 21-23) that any conservation principle, especially conservation of energy, confirms a specific prediction from the creation model. "The creation model predicts it! (The Second Law of Thermodynamics.)" If all these foundational laws of science were predicted by the creation model, why was so much time, energy, and resourcefulness required to discover them? Even if the assumption is made that these predictions are found in the Bible and were available before the discoveries were made, the predictions were certainly hidden from the discoverers. To claim to make predictions is to claim to declare in advance. *Scientific Creationism* fails to show that any specific prediction drawn from the creation model was directly responsible for leading any scientist to design a experiment or make an observation that made a contribution to the discovery of these very significant scientific concepts.

Scientific Creationism includes the excellent statement (p. 22) that "the universe is dynamic, forces are interacting, processes are taking place, events are happening, energy is being utilized and work is being done." Consistent with this statement, the book states (p. 25), "the fact that the universe is not yet dead is clear evidence that it is not infinitely old. Since it will die, in time, if present processes continue, time cannot have been of infinite duration." However, it also carries an assertion (p. 25) showing clearly that the author of *Scientific Creationism* has not comprehended either of these statements: "Therefore, the creationist would predict from the creation model that the stars and galaxies would *not* change, certainly not in any manner which would enable them to advance to higher levels in the hierarchy of stars. And the actual fact is that they have *not* so changed, thus conforming perfectly to the expectation of the creation model." This assertion of the unchanging stars is a medieval dogma that was shattered less than three years after Galileo first looked at the stars through a telescope. He discovered that the sun had spots that moved and changed. The sun is a star, but it is not an unchanging star. Galileo also discovered a nova, a star that suddenly becomes brighter. Clearly here was a star that changed. Stars are moving toward earth, stars are moving away from earth. Galaxies rotate in space. Many stars have variable brightness. To state as a fact that stars have not changed demonstrates a tremendous void in knowledge of astronomical observations made since Galileo, as well as meager insight into the meaning of the phrase, "The universe is dynamic."

On page twenty-six the statement appears: "It is obvious by definition that neither the big-bang theory nor the steady-state theory has any observational basis. In fact they contradict both Laws of Thermodynamics." While I can accept this assertion about the steady-state theory, the assertion is clearly false about the big-bang theory. Astronomers, thanks to the work of Edwin Powell Hubble, have been aware since 1929 that we live in an expanding universe. In 1948, George Gamow with Ralph Alpher and Robert Herman predicted the existence of a residual radiation from the initial big bang, and in 1964 Arno Penzias and Robert Wilson accidentally discovered the diffuse glow of this ancient radiation dating back to the birth of the universe some fifteen or twenty billion years ago. In 1990 COBE (NASA's Cosmic Background Explorer) provided 67 data points fitting a 2.735 K spectrum accurate to 1%. In 1992, COBE provided a visual image portraying the minute but very significant variations in this background temperature that verified the origins of structure in the universe at the moment the plasma became cool enough to become transparent. The specific historical steps of this discovery should not trouble creationists since it clearly substantiates the previously quoted creationist statement that the universe is not infinitely old.

An interesting study of how *Scientific Creationism* deals with phenomena is their treatment of the earth's magnetism. It states:

Phenomena such as these [accelerated radioactive decay rates] could be generated by such events as the reversal of the earth's magnetic field or super nova explosions in nearby stars. Since such phenomena are commonly accepted now as having occurred in the past, even by uniformitarian astronomers and geologists, there is a very real possibility that radioactive decay rates were much higher at various intervals in the past that they are at present. (p. 142)

On page 158, however, this statement appears: "Thus 10,000 years seems to be an outside limit for the age of the earth, based on the present decay of its magnetic field." How can the very well established periodic reversal of the earth's magnetic field be cited as a possible cause for accelerated radioactive decay and then a limit be placed on the earth's age based upon the decline of the field as observed during the past 135 years? Perhaps the field is preparing to reverse itself again in the near future! The quotation from page 142 raises three additional questions: Are there experimental data to verify modification of radioactive decay rates through exposure to magnetic fields? How is it that the unchanging stars explode? And finally, have geologists observed any evidence of the enormous release of energy that would have accompanied dramatically increased radioactive decay rates?

Another phenomenon that *Scientific Creationism* uses as evidence for a young earth is the influx of meteoritic material from space. The datum is presented (p. 152) that fourteen million tons of meteoritic dust settle on the earth's surface every year. Hans Pettersson is credited with announcing this measurement in an article that appeared in *Scientific American* in February 1960. Pettersson's 14 million tons per year is a speculative estimate based upon a questionable assumption: "If meteoric dust descends at the same rate as the dust created by the explosion of the Indonesian volcano Krakatoa in 1883, then my data indicate that the amount of meteoric dust landing on the earth every year is 14 million tons." I checked for more recent data in the 1967 edition of *World Book* encyclopedia and the 1974 edition of *Encyclopedia Britannica*. Both of these, and more recent references, estimated the amount of meteoritic dust settling on the Earth to be only as much as one thousand tons per day. This limit is based upon direct observations from space. Interplanetary dust particles are much rarer that had been anticipated (1). This upper limit is approximately 2.5% of the quantity cited in *Scientific Creationism*. Instead of two inches every five million years, less than one sixteenth of an inch of dust every five million years would have settled on the earth. This is not very convincing evidence to support the recent creation of the earth!

I taught physics. I expected the textbook I chose to aid me in teaching physics. I expected the textbook I chose to provide a reasonably accurate description of our modern era of science initiated primarily by Galileo. If contradictory material is introduced, this should be very clearly acknowledged. Highly speculative material should also be very clearly identified. *Scientific Creationism* fails to meet these very basic expectations. I served on several textbook committees evaluating physics textbooks. Each time I served I chose one textbook. Each time I rejected several textbooks. Some of the rejected books were nearly as good as the textbook selected. *Every textbook* I rejected contained better physics than *Scientific Creationism*.

References

1. NASA, 1981. **A Meeting with the Universe**, p. 57.

All material quoted, except Galileo's definition of inertia and Pettersson's statement, is from **Scientific Creationism** (Public School Edition) 1974, Creation-Life Publishers, San Diego, California. Galileo's definition is quoted from **PSSC Physics**, Fourth Edition, 1976, D. C. Heath and Company (p. 224).

Herman H. Kirkpatrick
Retired physics teacher
Roosevelt High School
Des Moines, IA 50317

SCIENTIFIC CREATIONISM

edited by Henry M. Morris
Master Books
El Cajon, CA (2nd edition, 1985)

This book comes in two editions, a "General Edition" and a "Public School Edition"; the former includes an additional chapter, entitled "Creation According to Scripture," which I will not discuss in this review. However, the "Public School Edition" is still filled with religious content, and is also thoroughly flawed and inaccurate in its scientific content; the book is inappropriate for use as a public school science textbook. It was prepared by the staff of the Institute for Creation Research, along with other consultants. Henry M. Morris (president of the ICR, and listed as the book's editor) appears to have been responsible for most of the writing.

The book represents the ICR's basic textbook of its so-called "scientific" creationism model, supposedly backed by scientific evidence but in reality based on a literal reading of Genesis: creation of the entire universe and all "kinds" of life only a few thousand years ago, with most of Earth's geology and fossil record created in a worldwide flood. The first seven chapters cover the range of issues in the creationism-evolution controversy: "Evolution or Creation?" (basic models and philosophical issues); "Chaos or Cosmos?" (origin of the universe and solar system); "Uphill or Downhill?" (thermodynamics, origin of life, mutations); "Accident or Plan?" (biological complexity, similarities, vestigial forms, embryology, the fossil record); "Uniformitarianism or Catastrophism?" (fossils and geology); "Old or Young?" (dating methods and the age of the Earth); and "Apes or Men?" (origin of humans, languages, religion, etc.).

Thus, the book attempts to cover a broad spectrum of scientific disciplines (physics, astronomy, chemistry, geology, paleontology, anthropology, etc.). However, its treatment of scientific knowledge in all of these is flawed. Rather than presenting the consensus of scientific experts in various disciplines, as we expect in a science textbook, Morris presents a mixture of non-expert or minority viewpoints, obsolete or discredited data, and other types of invalid information and conclusions. The experts have examined numerous claims made in this and other creationist works, and, as documented in many books and articles, have found them to be without scientific merit.

There are several types of errors and deficiencies in this book, which I will list along with only a few of the many possible examples:

Misunderstanding of the nature of science. While modern science does not claim to *prove* ideas, but rather to *support* them with evidence, Morris attacks evolution because it "cannot be proved" (pp. 5-6). However, evolution is accepted by science because it is extremely well supported by evidence. Thus, acceptance of evolution is not "faith" similar to religious faith (p. 69). Nor is evolution equivalent to a "religion, with its own system of ethics, values, and ultimate meanings," as claimed on page 196; science, including evolution, does not deal with these issues.

Appeal to religious prejudice. Morris attempts to prejudice his readers by stating that Christianity, Judaism, and Islam are "inherently creationist" (even though many believers in these religions also accept evolution), while Eastern religions, atheism, and humanism are linked to evolution (p. 16). He then goes on to group Marxists, Nazis (p. 16) and racists (pp. 179-180) among the believers in evolution.

Straw men. In many places Morris attributes to evolutionists ideas which they do not actually hold ("straw men"), and then refutes these ideas, as if this argues against evolution. Although a basic principle of science is that natural laws are constant, he claims (p. 18) that evolution predicts that these laws (such as the law of gravity) also evolve! Evolution recognizes that while mutations occasionally will be beneficial, they are more likely to be harmful; Morris claims that the "basic prediction" of evolution is that they will be beneficial, and proposes (p. 57) that evolutionists should favor increased mutations (such as from nuclear testing) in order to advance evolution. He devotes an extensive section (pp. 40-43) to refuting arguments supposedly offered for why the Second Law of Thermodynamics does not apply to evolution. But evolutionists do not make such arguments; there is no reason to, since experts in thermodynamics agree that evolution does not violate the Second Law (1). On pages 22 and 72, Morris suggests that according to evolution, we should expect a continuum of living things *in the present*, and thus be unable to classify organisms by their similarities and differences. However, evolution proposes that living things diverged *in the past*; with time, the differences have grown such that today we can observe distinct groups. Pages 59-62 are devoted to showing that the "probability of a complex system arising instantly by chance" is negligible, but scientists involved in origin of life research propose that complex systems arose step by step, not instantly. (Subsequent calculations (pp. 63-69) have other flaws, such as assuming that any failure destroys all progress; they are irrelevant to a scientific evaluation of whether life could have arisen by natural means.)

Misrepresentation of scientific knowledge. The text misrepresents the state of scientific understanding in several areas. On page 26, Morris states that "it is obvious by definition" that the Big Bang theory has no "observational basis." However, the theory was *based on* the observation that galaxies are receding in all directions at rates proportional to their distances; it predicted the cosmic microwave background radiation, which was later observed. On page 79, it is stated that "There is no evidence that there have ever been transitional forms" between basic "kinds." This is merely Morris's opinion; paleontologists believe that there is plenty of such evidence. On page 95, he says "The assumption of evolution is the basis upon which fossils are used to date the rocks." However, geology provides methods for determining the *relative* order of rock layers, and for using fossils to *correlate* layers of the same age in different locations. These do not require the assumption of evolution, and indeed were developed and applied by creationist geologists before Darwin's theory (2). *Absolute* ages are provided by radiodating, a later development which also involves no assumptions of evolution. On page 174, Morris suggests that the evidence for *Homo erectus* is "equivocal" for reasons such as the disappearance of the original Peking Man bones. However, numerous other specimens were known by the 1970s. (The revision of the book added a description of the

1984 discovery of a nearly complete *Homo erectus* skeleton, but left the earlier passage unchanged.)

Out-of-date material. The book's description of scientific knowledge, inadequate in 1974, has grown worse with time. Despite the many scientific advances from 1974 to 1985, the revised edition made minimal changes; new material was inserted where convenient (e.g., as footnotes or at ends of chapters), but very little of the text was rewritten. For example, while many precambrian animal fossils were known by 1985, Morris (p. 81) retained his reference (supported by quotes from the 1950s and 1960s) to the "tremendous gap" between one-celled organisms and Cambrian invertebrates. The evidence for continental drift has grown steadily stronger in recent decades, but a sentence expressing doubt about the evidence and stating that "the pendulum may be starting to swing back again" against the idea (p. 126) was left unchanged in the revised edition.

Since 1985, many new discoveries in various areas lend further support to evolution and refute the ICR's young-Earth and worldwide flood model, making the book even more out of date. For example, there has been an explosive growth in biochemical data (protein and gene sequences) supporting evolution. Morris (pp. 73-4) dismisses this type of evidence, claiming that it may illuminate "the true boundaries of the original created kinds," but in fact the data reveal the evolutionary unity of all living things.

Deceptive use of "catastrophism." Chapter V attempts to mislead the reader into thinking that the occurrence of catastrophic events supports creationism rather than conventional geology. Geologists have long recognized that catastrophic events were important in Earth's history; increasing attention to such events in recent years is not, as the book implies (p. 130), a consequence of "the rapid growth of the creation movement," but rather is the natural result of continuing research. Morris' catastrophism (which really involves just *one* catastrophic period, the worldwide flood and events in the subsequent centuries) bears little resemblance to that recognized by geologists, who have found evidence for numerous catastrophes over the 4.5-billion-year history of Earth.

Religious content. While the book supposedly uses only scientific arguments (except in the final chapter of the General Edition), it actually contains several theological arguments and thinly-disguised Bible stories. Morris comments on "the Creator's providential maintenance of the laws He created in the beginning" (p. 91), on why it would be inappropriate for the Creator to "waste aeons of time in essentially meaningless caretaking" (p. 136), and on the consequences of belief in "a personal Creator who had a specific purpose in his creation" (p. 178). A worldwide flood, which is based solely on the story of Noah and is refuted by the evidence of geology, is introduced in Chapter V to explain catastrophic geological events; by page 123, Morris discusses the "Flood" (capitalized) as if it were an established event. In Chapter VII we find the story of the Tower of Babel. While linguists, anthropologists, and archaeologists have no problem explaining the dispersal of humans around the Earth and the evolution of languages in terms of natural mechanisms, Morris claims (p. 185) that "there really seems no way to explain the different languages except in terms of the special creative purpose of the Creator," and on pages 187-8 reveals that this came about among descendants of "a remnant that survived the worldwide flood" as a result of "the Creator's direct creative restructuring of their common language into many languages."

Omission of opposing lines of evidence. Morris's treatment is also flawed by the omission of lines of evidence which argue against creationism. The area of biogeography (the geographical distribution of living and fossil organisms), which is considered one of the strongest areas of support for evolution, is not mentioned – perhaps because the data cannot be explained by the creationist post-flood dispersal (3). In discussing the supposed creation of Earth's geology in the worldwide flood, the book omits numerous features which cannot possibly have been formed in such a flood (e.g., fossil beaches and deserts; the layers of fossil forests in Yellowstone National Park; the Green River shales, where millions of annual layers of sediments can be observed) (4). The chapter on the age of the Earth does not mention the abundant astronomical evidence that the universe is very old (such as starlight that has been travelling for billions of years to reach us).

Double standards. In several cases the book applies far more rigorous standards to mainstream science than to creation "science." The pattern seen in the fossil record does not even remotely resemble that predicted by Morris's "cataclysmic model," and he admits (p. 120) that the model "would also admit of many exceptions in every case." However, he claims that "it is the exceptions that are inimical to the evolution model," even though science proposes reasonable explanations for exceptions such as those he cites. On page 129, Morris describes the handful of creationist scientists who have not yet had time to deal with the mass of geological evidence, as if we should admit "flood geology" into science classes based on our sympathy rather than on its scientific merits. The principles of carbon dating are well-supported, and the method can be calibrated against both historical evidence and tree-ring data, but Morris dismisses the latter because it "is highly subjective," and says that "it need not be considered further in this connection" (p. 193). However, he uses his own types of "corrections," which are not scientifically justified, to adjust radiocarbon ages of 8000- 9000 B.C. to about 3000-4000 B.C. (pp. 192-3).

Absurd conclusions. On page 117, Morris describes the worldwide flood as "a great hydraulic cataclysm ... accompanied by outpourings of magma from the mantle, gigantic earth movements, landslides, tsunamis, and explosions." Nevertheless, we are supposed to believe that in such turbulent and chaotic conditions, alternating flows of plant material and mud (p. 108) could neatly lay down the layers of coal seams – even a series of 50 to 60 cycles of sandstone, shale, and coal (p. 109). Morris concludes that his explanation is "much more realistic" than that proposed by geologists.

Inappropriate and misidentified sources. In a footnote on page 152, the revised edition updates an obsolete preliminary estimate of the influx of meteoritic dust with a newer reference, which supposedly gives an even higher value. However, this value comes not from the reference (erroneously listed as "1976," but actually from 1967), but rather from faulty calculations by an unidentified creationist (5). The real value, known since

1972 and confirmed by more recent data, is about 1000 times lower than that given by Morris, and is in accord with the amount of dust on the moon and its age of 4.5 billion years.

While scientists are aware of the possible errors in preliminary results (and news reports describing them), and thus give most weight to results described in regular peer-reviewed journal articles, Morris uses any type of material which seems to support his cause, such a story from *Science News* about a sculpture bearing "a vague resemblance" to *Archaeopteryx* as evidence that this animal was a contemporary of humans (pp. 121-2), and an abstract from a 1971 meeting allegedly casting doubt on carbon dating (p. 162).

Lack of scientific judgment. As evidence for the idea that humans and dinosaurs lived together, Morris describes the alleged human footprints among dinosaur prints at Paluxy River (pp. 122-3). However, experts have found the prints to be carvings, misidentified portions of dinosaurs prints, etc. (6); even the ICR was forced, in 1986, to admit that the evidence was questionable (7). The film "Footprints in Stone," recommended in the text, misleads the viewer by painting in the tracks to make them look more human-like; it was subsequently withdrawn from circulation. Morris's uncritical inclusion of the dubious Paluxy River material reflects a lack of scientific judgment.

Attacks on the honesty of scientists. On page 131, Morris states that for scientists who believe in evolution, any results which indicate that the Earth is young "must be explained away," an unfair attack on the integrity of the thousands of geologists who have dealt with these issues. Indeed, it is Morris who elsewhere wrote that since the Bible says the Earth is young, any dating measurements which give a great age "have somehow been misinterpreted" (8).

Use of discredited arguments. Many popular creationist arguments have been thoroughly refuted by scientific experts, yet Morris retained them in this book. One example is the decrease of the Earth's magnetic field, supposedly showing that the Earth must be young (pp. 157-8). However, it is well known that the magnetic field has gone through many cycles of increases and decreases over millions of years (9). (On page 142, Morris suggests that reversal of the earth's magnetic field might have altered radioactive decay rates, but on page 157 he claims that a creationist physicist "firmly refutes" the idea of magnetic field reversals!). Another example is three human fossils supposedly in the wrong strata (pp. 177). These actually consist of relatively modern bones buried in older strata, a misidentification by creationists of the actual strata, and a hoax (10).

Silly calculations. Perhaps the most absurd parts of the book are the calculations which purport to show that the Earth is young. Dividing the concentrations of chemicals in the ocean by the rate at which they enter from rivers (pp. 153-4) is an invalid method for determining the age of the Earth, since it ignores processes which remove the chemicals, and also assumes constant rates of influx (11). It is obvious that the method is flawed because the calculated "ages" are all different, and some are as small as 100 years! On pages 167-9, Morris assumes a constant growth rate for the human population to show that it could have reached its present level in just 4000 years, and that humans could not have existed for one million years. However, it is well known that the growth rate has increased dramatically in recent centuries. Moreover, calculations such as this generate ridiculously low numbers of people for ancient times (12).

No illustrations. This book is extraordinary for a science textbook in that it does not contain a single illustration, despite the many complex subjects it addresses.

Summary

Because of these many flaws, *Scientific Creationism* cannot be recommended for use in public school science classes, or indeed for anyone interested in learning science; it is essentially religious propaganda masquerading as science. It is, however, a valuable reference for anyone interested in studying the phenomenon of creationism.

References

1. Patterson, John W. 1983. "Thermodynamics and Evolution." In: L. R. Godfrey, ed., **Scientists Confront Creationism**, pp. 99-116. New York: W.W. Norton & Co.

2. Schafersman, Steven D. 1983. "Fossils, Stratigraphy, and Evolution: Consideration of a Creationist Argument." In: L. R. Godfrey, ed., **op. cit.**, pp. 219-244.

3. Cracraft, Joel 1983. "Systematics, Comparative Biology, and the Case Against Creationism." In: L. R. Godfrey, ed., **op. cit,**, pp. 163-191.

4. Weber, Christopher G. 1980. "The Fatal Flaws of Flood Geology." **Creation/Evolution** 1:24-37.

5. Wheeler, Thomas J. 1987. "More on Creationists and Meteoritic Dust." **Creation/ Evolution Newsletter** 7(4):14-15.

6. Cole, John R. and Godfrey, L.R., eds. 1985. "The Paluxy River Footprint Mystery - Solved." **Creation/Evolution** 15:1-56.

7. Morris, Henry M. 1986. Letter accompanying Institute for Creation Research **Impact** Number 151.

8. Morris, Henry M. 1972. **The Remarkable Birth of Planet Earth**, p. 89. San Diego: Creation-Life Publishers.

9. Dalrymple, G. Brent 1983. "Can the Earth be Dated from Decay of its Magnetic Field?" **Journal of Geological Education** 31:124-133.

10. Conrad, Ernest C. 1982. "Are There Human Fossils in the 'Wrong Place' for Evolution?" **Creation/Evolution** 8:14-22.

11. Dalrymple, G. Brent 1984. "How Old is the Earth? A Reply to 'Scientific' Creationism." In: F. Awbrey and W.M. Thwaites, eds., **Evolutionists Confront Creationists. Proceedings of the Annual Meeting, Pacific Division, American Association for the Advancement of Science** 1:66-131.

12. Milne, David H. 1984. "Creationist, Population Growth, Bunnies, and the Great Pyramid." **Creation/Evolution** 14:1-5.

Thomas J. Wheeler
Associate Professor of Biochemistry
University of Louisville
Louisville, KY 40292

THE SCIENTIFIC CASE FOR CREATION

by Henry M. Morris
Creation-Life Publishers
San Diego, CA (1977)

If you find James Hutton's two-hundred-year-old axiom of geology that "the present is a key to the past" plausible, you may have difficulty with *The Scientific Case for Creation*.

In this book the past must conform to a model of the universe recently created with perfect order, then subjected to entropy and a universal Flood, both being irreversible disintegrative processes. Thousands of extinct mammoths have been found along the shore of the Arctic Ocean. A few of these woolly mammoths have been found in a surprisingly well-preserved condition imbedded in ice. None of these fossils occur in marine deposits. *The Scientific Case for Creation* requires that all of these animals were drowned as the result of a single, universal Flood. Visitors to the Grand Canyon are able to view directly the exposed sequence of fossiliferous strata that forms a panorama several thousand feet thick in which the fossils all belong to extinct species. Each geological division has its own species not found above or below. *The Scientific Case for Creation* explains these observations as the result of the same single, universal Flood.

The Scientific Case for Creation provides no scientific evidence for the claim (p. 36) that: "There seems really no objective reason why the entire range of organic life preserved in the fossils could not have been living concurrently in one age." Fossils do provide evidence to the contrary:

1. Fossils generally can be identified and classified by detailed comparisons with other fossils and with living animals and plants.

2. Fossils are found where they are buried. Some are within layers of sedimentary strata. Some are in sandstone. Some are in hardened mud.

3. Fossils reflect varied environmental conditions, often unlike those existing today at the sites. The undisturbed debris of fresh-water swamp vegetation may alternate with seashells of marine life. Tropical palm leaves and crocodile bones are found at many places in the rocks of Arctic regions.

4. Fossils usually belong to extinct species. Only the shallowly buried examples are identical with or most like living species.

5. Fossil species are usually restricted to a limited part of the stratigraphic sequence. A few are longer lived. No species ranges throughout the whole sequence of strata. Individual species seldom disappear at one level and reappear at another layer.

The standard international stratigraphic system now in use by geologists was established in broad outline and was widely used by practical men searching for natural resources by 1840, nearly two decades before the publication of Darwin's theory of evolution. Stratigraphy was used to determine where coal and other fossil fuels could be found. The fossil sequence was not established to aid the argument for evolution.

Independent genetic evidence verifies relationships between species and provides supporting evidence for evolution. Knowledge of the fossil sequence and evolution reinforce each other but do not depend on each other. *The Scientific Case for Creation* portrays the fossil sequence and evolution as being mutually dependent, with geologists and biologists engaged in pure circular reasoning. The book ignores genetics, biochemistry, biogeography, etc.

The quality of radiometric dating is underestimated. Radiometric dating is cross-checked by independent laboratories, with different samples, by using more than one isotope pair. Highly concordant data differing by only one percent are not at all unusual. In spite of this high state of refinement of present day radiometric dating, *The Scientific Case for Creation* incorrectly asserts that evolutionists pick the age they want in the first place and then modify assumptions until the apparent age agrees with their wishes.

The Scientific Case for Creation is written by Henry M. Morris, author of many books, seventeen of which are listed in Books in Print in 1992. All of these are in the fields of scientific creationism and Christian apologetics. The purpose of all of his books is to support the belief that all Biblical assertions are historically and scientifically true, that the account of origins in Genesis is a factual presentation of simple historical truths, that all basic types of living things, including man, were made by direct creative acts by God during Creation Week as described in Genesis, that the great Flood in Genesis was a historical event, worldwide in its extent and effect. He claims to support this belief by scientific evidence.

If there is a scientific case for creation it should be presented to the scientific community in one of the recognized scientific journals or at one of the regularly scheduled scientific meetings. Sworn testimony by creationists at the 1982 Arkansas creationist/evolution trial (1) produced no evidence that any attempt had ever been made to pursue this well established process within the scientific community.

The Scientific Case for Creation is a book of Christian apologetics. It is not a reference book of science. It is on this basis that a determination for inclusion or exclusion in our public school book shelves should be made.

Reference

1. See "Creationism in Schools: The Decision in McLean versus the Arkansas Board of Education." **Science** 215:934-943 for the complete text of the judgement, injunction and opinion in the case.

Herman H Kirkpatrick
Retired physics teacher
Roosevelt High School
Des Moines, IA 50317

THE REMARKABLE BIRTH OF PLANET EARTH

by Henry Morris
Bethany Fellowship, Inc.
by special arrangement with Creation-Life Publishers
San Diego, CA (1978)

Henry Morris introduces *The Remarkable Birth of Planet Earth* as a book written to give "a brief summary of both Biblical and scientific reasons for believing in creation instead of evolution." Brief it is. In this short book Morris fails to mention most of the geologic evidence for an old earth, or the extensive genetic evidence for evolution. He makes no attempt to document numerous claims of fact which are not widely accepted.

As a reviewer I am compelled to provide the reader with background information which should be in the book. Accordingly, I must limit this review to a few representative topics.

The first chapter discusses probability arguments which "scientific" creationists regard as proving that evolution is impossible. Morris considers a skeleton of 200 bones and points out that the number of different ways to put together 200 bones is large (10^{375} or a 1 followed by 375 zeroes). He then points out that in 10 billion years there are only 10^{18} seconds, so it doesn't seem likely that random mutation could organize a skeleton.

Morris describes some counter arguments, but he never mentions the arguments a competent evolutionist would make. I will describe three.

First, consider this analogy: As I write this review there is weather outside. It is raining. According to Morris, this should come as a surprise because the probability of today's weather (a particular combination of temperature, humidity, atmospheric pressures, wind speed and direction, etc.) is so low. There are an infinite number of possible weather patterns. The probability of today's weather is not even one in 10^{375}; it is one in infinity, virtually zero. Nonetheless, there is weather because atmospheres must create weather even if any *particular* weather has no probability. Moreover, so many of these weather-patterns-with-no-probability happen to rain, that it makes sense to plant corn in Iowa.

In a similar way, living organisms are based on common properties of proteins. It is not surprising that an organism crawls, because proteins that change shape are as common as weathers that rain. The question is not whether some particular organism is probable, but whether the rules of biology create organisms. If there were only one skeleton that would work, evolution would be in trouble. However, there are trillions of skeletons that can work, just as there are trillions of weathers that can rain.

Morris picks the brain as a still more complex example of organization. "The cerebral cortex ... contains over 10 billion cells, all arranged in proper order ...." Of course, the question is not whether one proper order is probable, but whether some order that thinks is probable. As a matter of fact, it is easily shown that trillions of different memory networks can be composed of nerve cells whose connections are made completely at random.

The second point concerns a method of finding solutions to problems by trial and error. The method is called "gradient descent." Suppose we have a 200 bone skeleton with its head attached to its femur instead of its neck. Now suppose we make random changes in the skeleton and test its performance after each change. We do not keep any change unless it improves the performance. If one of these random changes connects the head to the scapula (shoulder), we will see an improvement in the performance of the skeleton. We will then begin making random changes to a skeleton which has its head attached to its scapula, saving only those changes which improve the performance. By this method we do not try all 10^{375} combinations. Any engineer can connect a 200 bone skeleton correctly with a couple thousand random changes. Gradient descent is exactly what evolution does. It tests every change.

Finally, an evolutionist must point out that the evolution of a skeleton does not really involve arranging 200 bones. It involves developing a segmented embryo (which gets all the vertebrae lined up). Then a few segments get limbs and some joints in each limb, but, frankly, it doesn't much matter how many or where.

Morris' second chapter begins by reminding us of the law of conservation of energy. He points out Biblical passages like, "By Him were all things created ... " (Colossians 1:16). We are to note that "created" is in the past tense, thus the law of conservation of energy. Morris then leaps to the great principle "that nothing is now being created or destroyed." The principle sounds fine when we first hear it because Morris agrees that the word "created" refers to creation out of nothing. The principle is presented as a statement of the laws of conservation of mass and energy.

Later, however, Morris uses this principle to conclude that species have not been created since the six day creation. In doing so he changes the meaning of the word "create" in the middle of his argument. It no longer refers to the creation of matter or energy out of nothing. It refers to the rearrangement of matter into new forms (species). Certainly, if there can be no rearrangement of matter, there can be no evolution, nor can I be putting ink on this page.

The remainder of the chapter covers the creationists' old argument about the second law of thermodynamics. As I have already discussed this issue in my review of S.E. Aw's *Chemical Evolution* in this volume, I will not do so again. However, I will observe that this section contains a good example of Morris' unique exegesis. His argument is simply this: God saw His creation was "very good." The second law requires that all motion in the universe will eventually decay into the not very interesting thermal motion of particles. It would not be very good to have such a Universe. Therefore, the second law must be a punishment for original sin, and not something present before the Fall.

Aside from the fact that the conclusion does not follow from the premises, it seems rather bold of Morris to impose his judgement as to what is good on the mind of God. In fact, there seems to be good reason to think that God does not intend this earth to last forever. The real question, of course, is why Morris bothers us with this strange exegesis which is entirely irrelevant to evolution.

The third chapter is a conventional creationist assault on the fossil record. The claims in this chapter have been thoroughly discredited. The arguments are too detailed to recount here; however, I will observe that creationists have had to defend the scientific basis of their claims in two landmark legal cases (*Aguillard v. Louisiana* and *McLean v. Arkansas*). In neither case did they mention the key claims that appear in this chapter.

The third chapter also incorrectly claims that a common method of dating fossils uses circular logic. The scientific argument is simple. Fossils appear consistently in the same order in sedimentary rocks from different locations. Fossils of more complex organisms are found nearer the surface of the sediments. This leads to the conclusion that the complex fossils are more recent. The corollary that rocks bearing similar fossils were formed at similar times is not circular.

Surprisingly little of the rest of the book has anything to do with evolution. It is largely given over to a complex exegesis which describes many supposed events in the creation of the universe. This seems to be an effort to make the Bible consistent with enough of science and history to prove its authority in areas where it is not consistent. The process is dubious in several ways. For example, it requires the reader to accept some unconventional definitions of words like "firmament" to circumvent otherwise obvious contradictions between the modern view of the universe and a literal reading of the Bible.

Morris' version of creation is as difficult to disprove as the claim that Bigfoot has tea with the leprechauns every Wednesday afternoon. However, difficulty in disproving something does not make it believable. Even if one foolishly grants all that Morris claims, both his exegesis and his "science" are left with major problems. He uses two finesses to deal with these problems.

First, Morris faces several points at which no exegesis can make the Bible consistent with the most fundamental science. He sweeps these away by asserting that the Bible is speaking figuratively in just these places. He also claims it is obvious when the Bible uses figurative language, and Genesis 1 is not figurative. It is easy to know when to take the Bible figuratively when you already know what conclusion you wish to reach. I am not prepared to accept Morris on his own authority.

Problems with his "science" are swept away by treating "uniformitarianism" as though it were a Biblical sin. "Uniformitarianism" is just the assumption that the laws of science don't change from day to day. An example of Morris' logic involves radioisotope evidence for the age of fossils. The only way around this strong evidence is to assume that the rate of isotopic decay changed at some time in the past. That's as drastic as claiming that gravity stopped for a week once but everything was held together by a sudden precipitation of super glue. Try to prove it never happened!

Instead of radioisotopic dating, Morris suggests we date the origin of man by extrapolating the current population growth backwards to 4000 BC. Talk about rampant uniformitarianism! We know perfectly well that the rate of population growth changes, and has been accelerating since the seventeenth century. (If we made the same extrapolation based on some species which is becoming extinct, the age of the earth would seem infinite.)

Morris' exegesis is interrupted by a discussion of the evolution of stars which is irrelevant to biological evolution but is a problem for "scientific" creationists because it also requires an old universe. Morris claims that the heavens are unchanged since the creation except for occasional novas. Novas, of course, are what stars produce when they are evolving from one stage to another.

This whole messy exegesis can be made unnecessary by some simple theology. The Bible just isn't about science; it's about religion. It is easy to understand Genesis 1 as a book about religion. At the time Genesis 1 was written, there were several religions directly competing with Judaism. They were polytheistic and had six day creation myths that were a lot like Genesis 1. The difference was that each creation was accompanied by the appearance of a new god. Genesis 1 takes us through the same story telling us, no, it was the one God and the one God again. Genesis 1 is not about science. It is about monotheism.

Finally, there are comments in the preface that need to be addressed. Morris promises to provide us with evidence for seventeen summary statements. In fact, he makes no effort to provide evidence for the last five. We must take them on his authority. I find them all offensive. Two of them read as follows.

15. Belief in evolution has historically been used by their leaders to justify a long succession of evil systems — including fascism, communism, anarchism, nazism, occultism, and many others.

Communists have not used evolution to justify their system. The Communist Manifesto was written more than a decade before *The Origin of Species*, and Soviet biology was held back for decades by Lysenko's refusal to accept the random nature of genetic change. (As a matter of rather obvious historical fact, the economic theory which has received the most spiritual support from the theory of evolution is capitalism.) It is probably true that racists have used the theory of evolution (just as they have used the Bible) to justify views they already hold. However, this misuse of evolution (and the Bible) has nothing to do with what is true, or with the morality of evolutionists.

16. Belief in evolution and animal kinship leads normally to selfishness, aggressiveness, and fighting between groups, as well as animalistic attitudes and behavior in individuals.

Not among the people *I* know.

I am thankful this is not my first review of a "scientific" creationist book. Previously, I was able to say of S.E. Aw's *Chemical Evolution* that the author is competent in his own discipline. I would like to be as kind to Henry Morris, but his theology is shallow; his exegesis is maddening; his science is wrong; and he tops it off by offending millions of Bible-believing Christian who also accept evolution.

David Vogel, Ph.D.
Department of Oral Biology
Creighton University School of Dentistry
Omaha, NE 68178

TRACKING THOSE INCREDIBLE DINOSAURS
And the People Who Knew Them
by John D. Morris
Master Books
San Diego, CA (3rd printing, 1984)

I recall on the banks of the Paluxy River near Glen Rose, Texas, during a sultry 1982 summer afternoon, being handed this book by a creationist friend of mine. For him it was printed justification of his enthusiasm for the claims that fossilized human footprints existed alongside those of dinosaurs along the banks of the river (thus sounding the death knell to evolution). And he was not alone. *Tracking Those Incredible Dinosaurs* was used for years by creationists to help them in battles over evolution in textbooks (1). For me it was a convenient and useful compilation of creationist man track claims along the Paluxy which helped launch many colleagues and me on our investigations of such claims.

My colleague Glen Kuban and I used Morris' book as a field guide to locate and study all the man track sites we could find in the years after the two of us met in 1984. *Tracking Those Incredible Dinosaurs'* large number of black and white photos are reproduced in sufficient detail to compare with actual features at the track sites. For those tracks not claimed by erosion over the years, its primary value remains as such a guide (though now superseded by such work as Kuban's (3,4)).

As an accurate description of what the alleged man track are, *Tracking Those Incredible Dinosaurs* fails miserably, belying the purpose encapsulated in its title. The line of man track investigators since 1980 have published detailed critical analysis of all phenomena claimed to be man tracks. Among these phenomena erroneously called human prints are erosional features, trace fossil patterns, carved fake prints, portions of poorly preserved dinosaur prints, and unusual dinosaur prints (1, 2, 3, 4). Yet Morris summarizes his interpretation of the information he has gathered thus: "If one allows the whole body of data to speak for itself ... the conclusion that man and dinosaur walked together at the same time and place ... seems inevitable" (p. 191). His "body of data" consists of eye-witness reports (e.g. pp. 28-42, 112-117, 124), poorly documented track sites (e.g. pp. 135, 141, 145, 156, 217, 222), and an uncanny ability to disregard or even mention plausible alternative explanations (e.g. pp. 140, 142, 203-221, 223-227, 228-233). One example of his detailed description that can be verified serves to question his reliability: the erosional features (many of which he describes as genuine prints — none are) on the Park Ledge in Dinosaur Valley State Park have not "eroded significantly in the last decade" as he claims, as shown by comparative photo analysis.

What does seem inevitable is Morris' unwillingness to publicly promote the identification of the best of the creationist alleged man tracks as infilled elongate dinosaur tracks, despite his being shown on site these saurian tracks very clearly in 1985 by Kuban (1,2); he has apparently no interest in clearing up the matter. Instead, the coloration showing clear saurian features of the very shallow tracks was questioned by Morris as possibly being fraudulently stained, so devastating was this phenomena to many man track enthusiasts (7). He had core samples made of the coloration boundaries, corings which Kuban and I essentially duplicated. Our corings showed clearly the coloration was a natural infilling phenomena going well below the surface (4, pp. 433-437). Morris' conclusion from his corings: "inconclusive."

Ironically, some of the photos in *Tracking Those Incredible Dinosaurs* reveal the very coloration phenomena that shattered the "best" creationist man track claims (including those of my creationist friend). Outlines of saurian digits are barely visible on photos of tracks H-1;-5, H-1;-2, H-1;-1, H-1; + 2, H-1; + 3, and H-1; + 4 on pages 204-205. The photo of H-1; + 3 on page 209 (another photo of which appears to be on page 88, though not identified as such) shows the same track used on the cover of the January 1987 *Journal of Geological Education* containing one of my publications identifying these particular "man tracks" as elongate, infilled dinosaur tracks.

True enough, the Institute of Creation Research (ICR) backed away from the man track claims in early 1986 through a letter written by John's father, Henry Morris, stating that the Paluxy prints could no longer be used as "evidence against evolution" (6). But since 1986 there has been no attempt by John Morris to clarify or rectify the incomplete and misleading description of the man track claims, which scientific scrutiny has shown *Tracking Those Incredible Dinosaurs* to contain. He has avoided all attempts I have made to communicate with him on this matter. Despite indications that this book would be taken off the market, it has apparently not been made unavailable (1). As a result, unless other more recent sources are sought out, something many of the creationist faithful are not known for, *Tracking Those Incredible Dinosaurs* unfortunately remains a cornucopia of misinformation to feed the credulous.

Among the latter-day credulous man track enthusiasts are supporters of Rev. Carl Baugh and Don Patton, who claim new evidence of man tracks *inside* the same elongate dinosaur tracks which were claimed as human until Kuban's and my work demonstrated otherwise. (Nothing new about this evidence, actually — merely erosional features of the infilling material of the shallow saurian tracks.) Morris and ICR have attempted to distance themselves from Baugh since 1986 with obvious good reason. Baugh and his associates have worked along the Paluxy since 1982, trying to uncover new man tracks, with no success — a decade of sporadic research at least partially inspired by *Tracking Those Incredible Dinosaurs*. Sadly, part of the book's legacy is undoubtedly the highly questionable methods, claims, and conclusions marking the work of Baugh and his associates (1, 2, 5).

References

1. Hastings, Ronnie J. 1988. "The Rise and Fall of the Paluxy Mantracks." **Perspectives on Science and Christian Faith** 40(3):144-155.

2. _____ 1987. "New Observations on Paluxy Tracks Confirm Their Dinosaurian Origin." **Journal of Geological Education** 35(1):4-15.

3. Kuban, Glen J. 1989a. "Elongate Dinosaur Tracks." In **Dinosaur Tracks and Traces**, David D. Gillette & Martin G. Lockley, eds. New York: Cambridge University Press. pp. 57-72.

4. _____ 1989b. "Color Distinctions and Other Curious Features of Dinosaur Tracks near Glen Rose, Texas." In **Dinosaur Tracks and Traces**, pp. 427-440.

5. _____ 1989c. "A Matter of Degree: An Examination of Carl Baugh's Credentials." NCSE **Reports** 9(6):15-20.

6. Morris, Henry 1986. Letter to friends of ICR, January.

7. Morris, John 1986. "The Paluxy River Mystery." **Acts & Facts**, Impact article No. 151. Institute for Creation Research, 2100 Greenfield Drive, El Cajon, CA 92021.

Ronnie J. Hastings, Ph.D.
High school science teacher
Waxahachie, TX 75165

WALK THE DINOSAUR TRAIL
Book 1, Trail's Beginning
by Barbara Sauer
Creation-Life Publishers
San Diego, CA (1981)

Introduction

The Teacher's Guide for this book states that there are two goals for the publication: 1) introduce the study of dinosaurs, and 2) expose the student to the creation/evolution controversy. I will review this book along these two lines. The book is an attractive paperback that appears to be at approximately the third or fourth grade level.

As An Introduction to the Study of Dinosaurs

Much has changed for students of dinosaurs. New discoveries and new methods of analysis call for replacement of the traditional view of these creatures as dull-witted brutes. The following are some of the areas in which advances in dinosaurian biology have been made:

1. **Physiology**: Classically viewed as sluggish, dinosaurs are now seen as very active organisms. Bone histology, predator/prey ratios, and functional anatomy of their locomotor systems indicate mammalian or avian activity levels (Bakker 1968, 1971a, 1972, 1980). This view is corroborated by speed analyses of trackways which indicate speeds of up to 50 miles per hour (Alexander 1976, Coombs 1978).

2. **Intelligence**: New analytic methods show that dinosaurs did not have exceedingly small brains. The ratio of brain size to body weight for most dinosaurs is the same as that for living crocodilians; and for some dinosaurs were at least as complex behaviorally as crocodilians and birds (Hopson 1977, 1980). Modern crocodilians have a wide behavioral repertoire, including advanced maternal and paternal care.

3. **Social Behavior**: New discoveries, and restudy of known trackway sites, show that herbivorous dinosaurs traveled in herds of at least 25 individuals, and that the youngest individuals were in the center of this herd (Bakker 1971b, Langston 1974). Other localities indicate that some carnivorous dinosaurs hunted in packs of 3-4 individuals. The study of newly discovered breeding grounds in Montana shows that dinosaurs returned year after year to the same areas to lay eggs, and that they nested communally (Gorman 1981, Horner and Makela 1979). Evidence from these sites also suggests parental care.

Even this short review shows that scientists now look at dinosaurs as highly active, intelligent organisms with complex social structure. In fact, the various dinosaur groups are better compared to large mammals (in terms of ecology) such as elephants, giraffes, etc., rather than crocodilians or lizards. This "new image" of dinosaurs has received quite wide publicity in magazines, books, and television. One book (Desmond 1976) was a Book-of-the-Month Club selection.

Thus it is surprising to me that none of this information appears in

Trail's Beginning. The discussion on page 15 of the text is flatly erroneous. *No scientist* has claimed that the dinosaurs were mammals, but rather that they had a mammalian level of activity. This is an important difference, and it indicates to me, along with the lack of the dinosaur's new image in this book, that Sauer did not carefully research her topic.

If the goal of this book is to introduce the student to the study of dinosaurs, then it clearly fails in its mission. It does not present up-to-date scientific information but rather a rehash of outdated material. By presenting the old and new models of dinosaurs, students could be shown how new discoveries and techniques lead to increased scientific knowledge. Sauer's book teaches neither how science functions nor what we now know about dinosaurs. Because of these failures I cannot recommend it for a science curriculum.

Presenting the Creation/Evolution Controversy

If this is the goal of the book, then all of the text is irrelevant. The text discusses dinosaur biology, none of which has anything to do with this controversy. Presenting this controversy would discuss such topics as: What is science? What rules do scientists follow? Is each model scientific? What predictions does each model make? Which model is falsified by the evidence?

Unfortunately, Sauer simply states that these two models exist and then drops the topic. To say that the creation model is scientific does not make it so. This book actually avoids the controversy which it purports to present.

Summary

This book fails to meet either of its stated goals and I cannot recommend its adoption for school use.

I have not had an opportunity to review either Book 2 or Book 3 in the *Walk The Dinosaur Trail* series. If in these other books, evidence for one model over the other is presented, then the scientific quality of such evidence must be assessed. However, if Book 1 is any indication of the quality of Sauer's research for her publications, then I would be very suspicious of any book she has written on scientific topics.

References

Alexander, R. McN. 1976. "Estimates of the speeds of dinosaurs." **Nature** 261:129-130.

Bakker, R.T. 1968. "The superiority of dinosaurs." **Discovery** 3(2): 11-22.

_____ 1971a. "Dinosaur physiology and the origin of mammals." **Evolution** 25(4):626-658.

_____ 1971b. "The ecology of the brontosaurs." **Nature** 229(5281): 172- 174.

_____ 1972. "Anatomical and ecological evidence of endothermy in dinosaurs." **Nature** 238(5359):81-85.

_____ 1980. "Dinosaur heresy — dinosaur renaissance: why we need endothermic archosaurs for a comprehensive theory of bioenergetic evolution." In Thomas, D.K., and E.C. Olson (eds.) 1980. **A Cold Look at the Warm Blooded Dinosaurs**. AAAS Selected Symposium 28:351-462.

Coombs, W.P. 1978. "Theoretical aspects of cursorial adaptations in dinosaurs." **Quaterly Review of Biology** 53(4):393-418.

Desmond, A.J. 1976. **The Hot Blooded Dinosaurs: a revolution in paleontology.** Dial Press, New York.

Gorman, J. 1981 "First of the red-hot mommas." **Discovery** 2(10):91-93.

Hopson, J.A. 1977. "Relative brain size and behavior or archosaurian reptiles." **Annual Review of Ecology and Systematics** 8:429-448.

_____ 1980. "Relative brain size in dinosaurs. Implications for endothermy." In: Thomas, D.K. and E.C. Olson (eds.) **A Cold Look at the Warm Blooded Dinosaurs.** AAAS Symposium 28:287-310.

Horner, J.R. & R. Makela 1979. "Nest of juveniles provides evidence of family structure among dinosaurs." **Nature** 282 (5736): 296:298.

Langston, W. 1974. "Nonmammalian Commanchean tetrapods." **Geoscience and Man** 3:77-102.

Daniel J. Chure
Park Paleontologist
Dinosaur National Monument
Jensen, UT 84035

The contents of this review are the opinons of Mr. Chure as a professional paleontologist and may not represent the views of Dinosaur National Monument, The National Park Service, or the Department of the Interior.

THE ORIGIN OF THE UNIVERSE
An Examination of the Big Bang and Steady State Cosmogonies

Technical Monograph No. 8
by Harold S. Slusher
Institute for Creation Research
Creation-Life Publishers
San Diego, CA   (1978)

I find this book of absolutely no pedagogical value whatsoever.

Much of the author's argument is based upon the Second Law of Thermodynamics, which, unfortunately, he does not understand. He argues that a young universe at high matter/energy density is in a state of disorder, while the present expanded universe is highly ordered. In this supposed transition from disorder to order he cites a violation of the Second Law. In fact the opposite is the case. A large container divided into two parts, with a gas filling one part while the other is empty, is a highly ordered system of low entropy. When the division is removed, the gas expands naturally to fill the container, moving to a state of greater disorder and of lower density, but of higher entropy.

If the author were simply incorrect in many of his arguments, then he might deserve kind treatment for his effort. However, I was shocked to discover many, many instances of apparent intellectual dishonesty. For example, he lists as a dilemma of cosmology the observation that the recessional velocity of clusters of galaxies increases with increasing distance. He remarks that this must indicate that we are located at the center of expansion. Now as someone who has at least read widely on the subject, he must be aware that the standard interpretation is one of uniform expansion, with no particular center. Not to mention this interpretation, but only to list the observation as a dilemma, is not candid.

As a second and final example I will cite, out of many possibilities, the author's statement that in the standard theory, many massive stars should already have evolved to white dwarfs; yet no massive white dwarfs have been found. Again, the author *must* be aware that the formation of planetary nebulae is just one of many mass loss mechanisms which explain why white dwarfs have substantially less mass than the stars from which they have evolved — a discussion which appears in any elementary astronomy text.

This author is guilty of selective rhetoric rather than rational discussion. Hence his book is not appropriate for use in science classes.

Lawrence P. Staunton
Associate Professor of Physics
Drake University
Des Moines, IA 50311

CRITIQUE OF RADIOMETRIC DATING

Technical Monograph No. 2
by Harold S. Slusher
Institute for Creation Research
Creation-Life Publishers
San Diego, CA (2nd edition, 1981)

The title of this booklet is quite inappropriate for what the author attempts to do in its writing. It is obvious to the reader from the start that the author is taking a strong stance on creationist faith. He is apparently bothered by the laws of radioactive decay, since these laws have led scientists to estimate the age of the earth to be billions of years.

The *Critique of Radiometric Dating* is actually an attack on evolutionary theory. The author states, "the evolutionist needs vast spans of time in the history of the earth." If one assumes that the earth has had a very short global history, "4000 to 10,000 years at most," then evolution could not have occurred. Hence, the radioactive decay laws, from which geological and historical dating have been done, must be shown to be in error. It appears that the author's purpose is to negate all the methods of radiometric dating so that his faith in creationism in not shaken.

The author does give an excellent description of the physics of radioactive decay. He clearly explains to lay readers the methods used to date geological and historical items. I could recommend this book to one looking for a brief description of radioactive decay chains and the mathematical equations used in converting half lives and isotopic ratios to years and ages. The Uranium-Thorium-Lead, Potassium-Argon, and Rubidium-Strontium methods are given special attention. Carbon-14 dating is also discussed as a method of dating historical events. One wonders how the author could present these clear descriptions without accepting their validity.

Instead of recognizing the accuracy within limits of the methods he describes, the author makes a feeble attempt to discredit them. He does this by exaggerating the experimental limitations of the dating methods, or by inventing or quoting other inventors of imaginary phenomena that may have caused the radioactive decay laws to be invalid. Such phenomena as a "vapor canopy," "shielding by a magnetic field," or "changes in atmospheric or cosmic ray condition" are suggested as reason why the radio time clocks cannot be relied upon.

In general, the author's criticism of dating methods consists of three main arguments.

1. No one now living observed conditions in the past, therefore we cannot know that the presently observed radioactive decay laws really hold over long periods of time. This argument cannot be refuted. However, the position would expect one to discard all truth deduced from observation of data. It discards the scientific method.

2. A second argument dwells on the uncertainty in the data, and uncertainty of the laws governing radioactive decay and geological aging. True, every measurement has an uncertainty. Every law is based on ob-

servation and there is always some uncertainty of the wholeness of the data. The author, however, fails to point out the correlation of the many methods of geologic dating. The author fails to state that carbon-14 dating was calibrated with known historical dates. True, extrapolation back in time is done, but the uncertainties in the dates are not such that one cannot distinguish between a billion or even a few million years and the mere "4000 to 10,000" years as claimed for the age of the earth by the author and some whom he cites.

3. A third argument is based on imagined or speculative possible environmental behavior that may have changed the rate laws for radioactive decay. A "shielding magnetic field," or "unusual cosmic rays" or "atmospheric changes" may have made the radioactive decay rates different in other ages. In fact, no known natural phenomena have been observed to change the decay rate, with the possible exception of K-capture. Vapor changes and electromagnetic changes occur in the 10 to 1000 electron volt energy range, whereas nuclear change requires the million electron volt energies. Of course, some cosmic ray energies are that high, but there is no known evidence for great cosmic ray fluctuation in the past few thousand years.

In summary, the *Critique of Radiometric Dating* by Harold Slusher is a feeble attempt to make the reader believe that radioactive decay constants are not constant. He completely fails in his attempt to prove that the earth is only four to ten thousand years old, dates that seem to satisfy his creationist faith. This book is clearly not appropriate for use in a contemporary science class.

Joe D. Woods
Professor Emeritus of Chemistry
Drake University
Des Moines, IA 50311

THE EYE
A Light Receiver

by Wilburn B. Sooter
Creation-Life Publishers
San Diego, CA (1981)

This 28-page paperback is intended for elementary school science classes. It was produced as part of a writing project sponsored by the Institute for Creation Research and directed by Richard B. Bliss. An "Introduction to the Student" sets forth the book's objectives: To enable the student-reader to choose between a creationist and an evolutionary interpretation of the function of the eye. The chosen objective appears to be presumptuous and unrealistic; and there is nothing in the book that would help the reader to make an *informed* judgment as between the two "models" that the Introduction offers.

The Introduction also refers to a 1978 "study" that purports to validate the two-model pedagogical approach. (Presumably the "study" is an investigation that Bliss conducted while science consultant to the Racine school system, and that he submitted to the University of Sarasota in partial fulfillment of the requirements for his Ed.D. degree.) Of course, such vague mention of a "study" is hardly acceptable as a scientific reference. It is also unclear what significance this trivial discussion of pedagogical methodology has for elementary school children.

The two models are discussed explicitly in boxes on page 21. The creation item concludes: "The evidence from observation and facts supported the intelligent creation of the eye" (the familiar "argument from design"). The evolution item concludes: "This supports the random evolution of the eye." Note in this latter statement the loaded word "random," which only a creationist would use in this context. The two statements add up to slick propaganda for creationism, reinforced by a creationist slant throughout the book.

The descriptive material on the structure and function of the eye is rather pedestrian, but in general acceptable. Some of the language tends to be sloppy: "People are able to see equally in all directions" (p.6). The scientific content is also somewhat marred by heavy personification: a "special light beam named Mr. Light Ray" is pictured on almost every page and gets awfully cute before we reach the end of the book. An appendix gives directions for some simple, standard investigations of visual functions: fusion of visual fields, location of the blind spot, accommodation, pupillary reflex. Pedagogically this is the most valuable section of the book, and it is likely to be the most interesting to students.

A glossary lists key terms with definitions — many of them very poor: "decode: to give understanding," "evolution: the idea that simple life forms can change to complex ones over long periods of time," "scientist: a person learned in science." A list of "Resource Books" appears more impressive than useful. One wonders how appropriate the *Illustrated Medical and Health Encyclopedia* by Morris Fishbain [*sic*] and a tape by an ear, nose, throat, and plastic surgeon are for elementary schools.

Despite the limitations just pointed out, the book would be marginally acceptable except for its heavy bias toward creationism. Use for propaganda purposes of a legitimate study of the eye is not proper. Nor is it good science teaching to ask students to make judgments without adequate information, comprehension, and maturity. Finally, teaching religious concepts in the guise of science, as Sooter attempts to do here, makes his book, *The Eye*, constitutionally unacceptable for public school use.

Bob Vanden Branden
Retired, Drake University
Des Moines, IA 50311

DARWIN'S ENIGMA

by Luther D. Sunderland
Master Book Publishers
El Cajon, CA (1984)

A good portion of this book deals with personal interviews that the author had with certain evolutionary scholars. Consequently, reviewing the book presents a bit of a problem because the quotations that he ascribes to those scholars cannot be easily confirmed for accuracy. However, the author does use many of the standard creationist arguments in an attempt to prove his case, usually in a manner that would prove effective in influencing the uninformed reader. Some of those arguments will be addressed here.

As do many other creationist authors, Sunderland makes much of some statements that Professor Karl Popper made concerning evolution, specifically that to be scientific a theory must be testable. Sunderland asserts that Popper indicated in some of his writings that evolution was not testable and therefore not a valid scientific theory. However, Popper was specifically speaking of the theory of natural selection and not evolution per se. Moreover, Popper subsequently stated that he was wrong concerning the testability of natural selection, something that Sunderland fails to note.

Of Fred Hoyle and Chandra Wickramasinghe, Sunderland stated, "According to their calculations, the probability of life originating by random processes was one chance in 10^{40000}." In fact, these two did not say that. What they said was that the chance of obtaining in a random trial the 2,000 enzymes found in life forms on earth is one part in 10^{40000}.

However, Hoyle and Wickramasinghe themselves did not accurately state the problem. Their argument was made after the fact. It is like saying that those gentleman in the back room could not have played poker last night because the odds were astronomical against the purported sets of hands having been dealt. Of course, the odds against any *particular* set of poker hands being dealt is astronomical, but that does not prevent someone from playing poker. A poker player plays with whatever hand he is dealt, however unlikely it is for any *particular* hand to be dealt. As with the possible number of poker hands, there is a virtual infinite number of possible enzymes, and there was no before-hand requirement that the particular 2,000 enzymes be used. Life on Earth used, and modified, whatever enzymes it was dealt. In fact, of the astronomical number of possible, but non-occurring enzymes, many would certainly be more efficient than the ones that are actually found here on Earth. On other planets, completely different sets of enzymes would be dealt, and life on those planets would evolve accordingly.

Sunderland notes that evolutionists argue that homology — i.e. similarity of structures in different species — implies an evolutionary relationship. He tries to show that homologous structures do not necessarily indicate an evolutionary relationship, but he uses improper, irrelevant, and often erroneous examples, many of which ignore the principle that similar structures in different species cannot be looked at in isolation, but must be examined in relation to the overall structures of the organisms in question.

For example, Sunderland argues that the eye of the octopus is similar to that of man, but that the two species are obviously not closely related, and therefore the principle of homology is invalid. However, the similarity of the eyes in the two species is actually an example of convergent evolution and is the result of the constraints of the laws of optical physics. Imaging structures using a lens would have to be similar in unrelated species because of those laws; otherwise the structures would not be functional or would function inefficiently. Moreover, the nerve ganglions picking up the signals from the retina are in front of the retina in the human eye, but are behind the retina in the octopus (which is actually a better "design"). This indicates that the eyes in these two species evolved independently.

Repeating a standard creationist argument concerning homology, Sunderland also said that the milk of the ass is similar to that of humans. But, of course, it is to be expected that there will be some similarity because both species are mammals. However, human milk proteins are in fact more similar to those of macaque milk than of donkey milk (as should be the case according to the evolutionary relationship) and human and chimpanzee milk lysozymes are identical (as again should be the case).

Quoting the British evolutionist, Gavin de Beer, Sunderland goes on to assert that homologous structures are not controlled by homologous genes. As William Thwaites has shown, this argument is erroneous. De Beer's conclusion was actually a question and was based on genetic experiments with fruit flies. However, a contemporary geneticist would understand that the problem de Beer noted was likely caused by "suppressor" mutations. The "missing" gene that was supposed to control a structure was not really missing, but merely suppressed and could express itself again as a result of a mutation that counteracts the suppressor mutation.

As is frequently the case in creationist literature, Sunderland argues that the fossil record does not support evolution because of the lack of transitional forms. According to him the fossil record would be best explained by a catastrophe, such as a world-wide flood. And, as is typical in the creationist literature, Sunderland makes no reference to the fact that, if such an event did occur, all species, extinct and extant, would be found throughout the fossil record. Instead, of course, we find that, for example, no fossils of modern, present-day mammal or bird species are found in association with dinosaur fossils in any deposits anywhere in the world, but are always found in younger strata. Similar situations exist for other groupings of species. The fossil record, of course, is best explained by an evolutionary process.

Sunderland makes many other standard creationist arguments against evolution, often in a more effective manner than by most other creationist writers. However, these arguments have been addressed and answered before and need not be covered here.

David Persuitte
Author, Technical editor
Arnold, MD 21012

THE MYSTERY OF LIFE'S ORIGIN
Reassessing Current Theories

by Charles B. Thaxton, Walter L. Bradley and Roger L. Olsen
Philosophical Library
New York (1984)

On its cover, *The Mysteries of Life's Origin* is called "a book favorable to creation — from a publisher not even sympathetic to it," and given "solid marks for excellence" by "numerous scientists." I took the bait, and indeed had my curiosity satisfied.

Although not suitable as a science text, the book is well worth reading for several reasons. It is such a refreshing departure from the usual mix of Bible quotes, authoritarian references, defamation of evolution, and scientific terminology typical of creationist literature, especially that of Henry Morris, Duane Gish or Walter Lang. There is no direct religious appeal or even subtle Christian evangelism, and purposely so. The theme is a survey of biochemical research into life's origins over the past three decades or so, which is interpreted as failing to account for the origin of life. Even the departure from science at the end of the book is subdued and in the main unassuming. Of particular interest to those interested in the variety of present creationist claims is what appears to be assent to an earth billions of years old. A universal flood is not mentioned, as if it had no role at all. The sustenance of life is seen as understandable in terms of the physical laws of biochemistry and thermodynamics, all in accordance with the Second Law of Thermodynamics, and all generally and remarkably in accordance with uniformitarianism. I am reminded that my attention as a physicist, early on, was drawn to creationists' claims by their persistent misunderstanding and/or use of the Second Law concerning living systems. This book clearly is a welcome departure from that pattern. Only the origin of life is seen as not accounted for by these laws (though there is no definite assent to evolutionary mechanisms after the appearance of life). After reading this book and comparing it with other creationist works, I thought, "Yes, Virginia, there *are* intelligent creationists!"

The authors see themselves as long-overdue critics of the assumptions and interpretations of scientific origin-of-life research, even though none of them is a specialist in such research (Thaxton was a chemist and curriculum director for the Foundation for Thought and Ethics, Bradley is a mechanical engineering professor, and Olsen was a geochemist and project supervisor for a waste management service). They say, "There are times, however, when workers with specialized knowledge in overlapping disciplines can bring new insights to an area of study, enabling them to make original contributions." Though such contributions "from the outside" are indeed possible, none of the authors' professional work is cited as relevant to their points. Anyone can criticize, as I am doing here, but to make "original contributions," it would seem that actual biochemical research adding to the present data base would be a minimum requirement — rather than merely selective library research. In the foreword, Dean Kenyon states, "It is very likely that research on life's origins will move in somewhat different directions once the professionals have read this important work." However, given the criticism which makes up most of this book, which is virtually free of scientific suggestions, it seems highly unlikely that scientific origin-of-life research will be given new directions by this work.

Thaxton is a proponent of the rather odd philosophical dualism of distinct laws of origins (origin science) added to traditional laws of operation (operation science) espoused principally by Norman Geisler of Dallas Theological Seminary. This dualism is actually a latter-day version of the argument from design. Though Thaxton has recently regretted this dualism, William Thwaites some time ago pointed out that such a distinction of different sciences is neither obvious nor needed. What appears to be "operation science" is that which does not offend creationist sensibilities, and what is called "origin science" tends to offend such sensibilities, much like "horizontal" (intra-species) evolution does not offend modern creationists, while "vertical" (inter-species) evolution does. Bradley's forte is the inadequacy of naturalistic ways of accounting for life's origins (1). Thaxton and Geisler seem to have difficulty with the historical inquiries of science since the birth of geology, and Bradley seems uncomfortable with the naturalistic foundations of the philosophy of science. Using these difficulties as a springboard, the inclusion of a Creator in science is seriously espoused as necessary.

The authors maintain that "the *source* of our initial assumptions is of little import" [emphasis theirs]. But I strongly disagree, since knowing the philosophical views of Thaxton and Bradley can be extremely helpful in explaining why their sources and very selective and incomplete. For instance, they rely heavily upon the work of H. P. Yockey without regard to the inapplicability of Yockey's calculations and the errors in his conclusions (2, 3, 4). When they cite the susceptibility of substances to processes such as hydrolysis — contending therefore, that the prebiotic soup is a "myth" — they fail to emphasize the resistance and stability of many biochemical structures. That gene duplication accounts for complexity, and the selection pressures of active self-replicating structures, also seem ignored. The authors should heed their own words from Chapter 11: "In the persuading process there is always the risk that partial truth will be viewed as the whole truth and mislead a jury."

In February, 1985, the three authors were joined by Kenyon and Yockey to form a panel of theists in a discussion on the origin of life (5). The non-theistic panel included Russell Doolittle, Donald Goldsmith, Robert Shapiro, William Thwaites, and Clifford Matthews. Bradley had informed me previously that the book had already been helpful in Matthews' research at the University of Illinois at Chicago. After the panel discussion, I asked Matthews if this were true, and he said only as a critique of origin-of-life laboratory research in the past. Bradley had to concur with its usefulness only in this sense. I must say that I would expect much more from an "important" work destined to provide "somewhat different directions" in scientific research! Pointing out problems, admittedly a vital and valuable service in science, is hardly a turning point, a breakthrough, or a new insight leading to new directions in research.

To their credit, the authors admit they are fallible. In the preface they state, "Even if our critique is shown to be deficient and the chemical evolution scenario is vindicated, perhaps the present work will have played a role in goading scientific workers into presenting a clearer and stronger defense in its behalf." Perhaps, but what this work did for me as a layman in the field of biochemistry was to demonstrate the enormous achievements that have been made in the past thirty years in origin-of-life research, from Stanley Miller's first amino acid synthesis to Sidney Fox's protocells. (If only research toward controlled fusion had had similar success in the same time period!)

To their discredit, the authors would have their readers believe that origin-of-life research is full of exaggerated speculation and in a state of crisis. Given our leaps of knowledge in biochemistry, such as the chemical structure of DNA and RNA, such seems more wishful thinking than description.

To me the real message of the book is in the epilogue. For here is where the authors, on the basis of the inadequacy of naturalistic explanations they feel they have established in the previous chapters, call for the inclusion of metaphysical considerations under the guise of "origin science." David Bohm and others are used to justify this suggestion, but a supernatural deity, indistinguishable from the Judeo-Christian variety, is soon made the preferable form of their metaphysics. Though openness to any theistic view is implied, the rest of the epilogue comes across as Christian apologetics, disguised though it may be, in the Morris and Gish tradition. If this is their "original contribution," there is nothing original, much less scientific, in it at all. I realize that I was forewarned by the book's advertising, but I still felt let down by this lack of scientific content at the end, given its presence in the rest of the book.

At least one glaring omission in the epilogue serves to emphasize that the message of the book is religious apologetics, not philosophy of science or desire to genuinely contribute to science. From many alternatives, including panspermia, special creation by a Creator external to the cosmos is billed as the most plausible way to account for life's origin, assuming that the naturalistic biochemical explanation is indeed inadequate. But what about the possibility of "unnatural" origins of life, wherein unknown processes of matter and energy bring about the appearance of life as we know it and then disappear without a trace? In this scenario, life, once established, becomes subject to uniformitarianism, evolution, and thermodynamics. No deity, supernatural or otherwise, is required. Applying Occam's Razor, this scenario "saves an assumption" and is thereby philosophically preferable to one in which the characteristics of a deity or Deity are blended. The latter approach creates problems which give even theologians headaches. Bradley's rejoinder to my suggestion was that no one seriously takes this position in the philosophy of science, presumable due to the inaccessibility of "unnatural" laws or origin. No one would seriously want to include a supernatural deity on the philosophy of science for similar reasons.

As atypical as the creationist sympathies in this book may be, the very small part of the epilogue which is theology resembles the very problematic theology I think is characteristic of so much of today's creationism. A supernatural deity is invoked when ignorance or, in this case, alleged failure to rationally account for phenomena is encountered. This is but a God-of-the-gaps theology in which God is associated with the absence of knowledge, and God retreats before the growth of knowledge. Speaking again as a layman, this time in theology, it appears to me that this God is not consistent with much of Scripture and most of orthodox Christianity.

Through their metaphysical additions, the authors in effect are calling for a redefinition of science. With their particular and highly selective version of metaphysics, however, this redefinition undermines one of the great strengths of science — its coherent practice across the world's vast and varied religions, politics, and creeds. Whatever may or may not have been the role of metaphysics in inspiring ideas in science, what is included in science is in itself as independent of metaphysics as is humanly possible. It is critical to remember that science is one area in which theists, atheists, agnostics, pantheists, and even creationists can and do agree.

In conclusion it seems clear that the authors of this book, in their epilogue, are asking science to do something it cannot do without losing its identity, as if they were asking basketball to be played with the rules of baseball. Science has no other alternative than to approach the question of origins from a uniformitarian and positivistic perspective. Science is equipped to explore the question of origins assuming matter and energy give rise to life and intelligence, not assuming there was an intelligence giving rise to matter and energy. To invoke a deity, to assume any form of supernaturalism, or even to postulate unknowable and unnatural laws is to do something other than science. Science could well be looked upon as a search for naturalistic answers to questions about reality — to see how far naturalistic assumptions will allow us to probe. Surely it is incredibly remarkable, and one of the wonders of science, to realize just how far into reality naturalism, dynamic and flexible as it is, allows science to peer.

References

1. Bradley, Walter L. 1980. "Thermodynamics and the Origin of Life," Probe Ministries International.

2. Doolittle, Russell F. 1983. "Probability and the Origin of Life." In **Scientists Confront Creationism**, Laurie R. Godfrey, ed. New York: W.W. Norton.

3. Doolittle, Russell F. 1984. "Some Rebutting Comments to Creationists' Views on the Origin of Life." In **Evolutionists Confront Creationists**, Frank Awbrey and William M. Thwaites, eds. San Francisco: AAAS, Pacific Division.

4. Thwaites, William M. 1984. "An Answer to Dr. Geisler — From the Perspective of Biology." **Creation/Evolution** XIII:13-20.

5. Panel discussion centering on the origin of life, "Christianity Challenges the University: An International Conference of Theists and Atheists," sponsored by Dallas Baptist University and The Institute for Research in Christianity and Contemporary Thought. February 7-10, 1985, Dallas.

This review is a revised version of one originally published in the *Creation/Evolution Newsletter* 5(1) in 1985, and is reprinted by persmission.

Ronnie J. Hastings, Ph.D.
High school science teacher
Waxahatchie, TX 75165

THE HISTORY OF EVOLUTIONARY THOUGHT

by Bert Thompson
Apologetics Press
Fort Worth, TX (1981)

In scientific circles creationists are well known for re-writing science. Now Bert Thompson has the dubious honor of trying to re-write history. This book presumes to be a brief history of evolutionary thought, but instead it is a biased attack on evolution and on historical figures within the scientific community. When it is descriptive rather than derogatory, it is a boring recitation of dates and names, derived almost exclusively from secondary or tertiary sources. Rather than develop a logically or empirically compelling argument of his own, Thompson consistently adopts the typically creationist ploy of searching the literature for just the right quotations (many of the same ones used by other creationists) to express his viewpoint. In the last chapter Thompson abandons all pretense of writing history and launches a frontal assault on evolution, focusing particularly on the roles therein of mutation and natural selection. The chapter is a "critique" consisting entirely of a long list of quotations, including even Alexander Graham Bell among the sources! The entire book reads like a high school term paper.

The book opens with short vignettes of historical figures concerned with evolution, from the Greeks to the early twentieth century. These are followed by chapters on the Scopes trial, on the recent legislative controversies involving creation/evolution, and a final chapter on neo-Darwinism and the "modern synthesis." Exemplary scholarship clearly is not one of the goals of this book. Except for very recent works, primary sources are rarely used. Indeed, the most used sources are writings by other creationists. Judging by the number of quotations from Henry Morris's *The Troubled Waters of Evolution*, this must be Thompson's favorite book. There are many excellent and easily accessible studies on the history of evolutionary thought, but Thompson cites none of them.

Typographical and factual errors are too numerous to list in full. The table of contents lists two Chapter Three's. George Gaylord Simpson was not deceased in 1981 (p. 52). Richard Owen was not "one of Cuvier's most distinguished pupils." The biogenetic law is not in disrepute; only Haeckel's capsule version of it, "ontogeny recapitulates phylogeny," has been replaced. And so on.

What is far more serious, of course, is the way in which Thompson re-writes history to suit his own fundamentalist position, Alfred Russell Wallace's view of evolution, for example, was not rejected in favor of Darwin's because the former had religious beliefs and the latter had none, but because Wallace's science was not as acceptable as Darwin's, and because Wallace was not a member of the Victorian scientific establishment while Darwin was.

To Thompson, those who oppose evolution are "powerful writers," "brilliant," "distinguished," and so forth, while such superlatives are limited when evolutionists are mentioned. Nor does he restrict this method of argumentation to science. Thus in the discussion of the Scopes Trial the prosecution attorneys for the defense, Clarence Darrow, is also "renowned," but only as a "criminal lawyer and agnostic ... a favorite defense attorney for known criminals." Mr. Thompson clearly does not like the efforts of the American Civil Liberties Union to establish the constitutional right of freedom of religion, and he expresses that dislike by claiming that the ACLU defended Scopes solely in order to attack the Bible and Christianity. In support of this claim he cites one creationist writer, and one "Christian" newspaper dating from 1925. So much for historical objectivity.

But the most outrageous historical misinterpretation Thompson saves for poor Darwin himself. Using a bit of selective quotation, Thompson tries to make Darwin out a rather mediocre scientist who happened to push an idea (which was wrong, of course) that was accepted only because it fit in with the anti-religious feeling of the day. It is not Darwin's mediocrity that is brought into question here, but Thompson's. The volume and the quality of Darwin's research gained him recognition as a first-rank scientist before he ever published a word on evolution. Darwinism spread because it offered a *scientific* (i.e. naturalistic) explanation for the diversity of life. To be sure the time was ripe; yet scientists of the day were not rejecting religion, rather they simply were casting off supernaturalism as a basis for scientific explanations. Unlike Thompson and his fellow creationists, these scientists wanted to practice science, not theology.

Ironically, one of Thompson's own creationist quotations provides the appropriate epitaph for this book: "It is unfortunate that the public is more willing to accept an entertaining fictionalization of history than to exert the effort to find out alternate versions for themselves ..." (p. 163). How true, Dr. Thompson, how true.

A book as heavily biased and as grossly inaccurate as Thompson's is not calculated to give students any real understanding of the history and nature of science. The book does not belong in any self-respecting school.

Joel Cracraft
Department of Ornithology
American Museum of Natural History
New York, NY 10024

SCIENCE HELD HOSTAGE

by Howard J. Van Till, Davis A. Young, and Clarence Menninga
InterVarsity Press
Downers Grove, Illinois (1988)

Editor's Note: *This is not a "creation science" book as most of the others reviewed here are. However, the authors are evangelicals, and they do address the issue of "scientific" creationism — albeit in a very different way from the others. Thus a review of it seems well worth including.*

The three authors of *Science Held Hostage* are all conservative Christians and professors of the physical sciences at Calvin College, Grand Rapids, Michigan. The college itself is also theologically conservative. There, shortly before publishing this book, its authors survived a heresy investigation incited by, among others, Duane Gish of the Institute for Creation Research. Van Till is an astronomer. Young and Menninga are geologists. All three are competent expositors of their fields.

Their book is a sustained and successful attempt to identify the proper boundaries of science. Their motive in writing it appears to have been to protect both science and their own Christian worldview, first from the disreputable arguments of fellow Christians who call themselves "creation scientists," and then from reputable scientists who fail to make necessary distinctions between their own naturalistic worldview, extrapolated from science, and the more limited enterprise of science itself.

Part I of the book, "Science as Practiced by Scientists," usefully discusses the concerns and characteristics of science, and thus its boundaries.

The four chapters of Part II, "Science Held Hostage by Creationism," present four case studies, in fields of the authors' expertise, of claims made by "creation scientists" in support of their young-earth scenario. These include "the legend of the shrinking sun," the claim that an old moon should have more dust on it, the claim that an old earth should have saltier oceans, and the claim that the Grand Canyon provides evidence for flood geology and against the standard understanding of the geologic column. Each of these case studies is a devastating critique of "creation science." In each case, creationism's greatest sin is shown to be ignoring, or even denying the existence of, evidence that refutes it.

The analysis of creationist claims about the Grand Canyon is especially valuable because the geologic time scale is central to the interpretation of earth history, and the creationist rejection of that time scale is central to "creation science." For example, creationists allege that the Grand Canyon provides evidence that layers of Mississippian age were deposited immediately after layers of Cambrian age, without interruption. The authors of this book show that there is plenty of evidence for interruption — and for the intervening Ordovician, Silurian, and Devonian periods.

Early in Part III, "Science Held Hostage by Naturalism," it says, "many recent books written in defense of organic evolution and in opposition to scientific creationism are commendable for their careful avoidance of using natural science as a tool to attack religious belief. The domain of science is generally understood and respected." As examples, they cite books by Norman Newell, Niles Eldredge, Michael Ruse, and Philip Kitcher.

By contrast, they dispute the claim they attribute to Isaac Asimov's *In the Beginning*: that science "ultimately has the power to determine whether or not a theistic, deistic or atheistic world view is legitimate." They accuse him of having "incorrectly transposed the *methodological* naturalism of professional natural science into a universal *ontological* or *metaphysical* naturalism."

This terminology helps make an important distinction. If it is the goal of science to build descriptive and conceptual structures that appeal to well-informed and rational people everywhere, then scientists must avoid invoking untestable components in their explanations. Supernatural concepts, even if true, have no place in science because they are inherently untestable. The same is true of statements that deny the reality of supernatural concepts. To achieve its goal, science must forfeit its power to make claims that might be true but that cannot be substantiated adequately. It must stick to arguments that are compelling. Flights of imagination, extrapolation, and interpretation should be clearly labelled as such. To be able to speak convincingly about some things less than ultimate, science forgoes the privilege of making claims about the ultimate nature of reality. Its naturalism is methodological, not ontological.

The authors have generally high praise for Douglas Futuyma's *Science on Trial*, but they quote and analyze four passages that exemplify "unfortunate language" that might cause "an undiscerning reader [to] be strongly inclined to draw metaphysical conclusions from science."

The authors devote a chapter to challenging P. W. Atkins's book, *The Creation*, the dust jacket of which, they say, promises readers that they will "discover both the ultimate nature of the universe and the manner in which it came into being." The authors say Atkins is entitled to profess his naturalistic creed, but his conclusions do not follow, as he implies, logically and necessarily from science. They give him "credit" for showing that a consistently naturalistic perspective leads to seeing existence as utterly meaningless. Since they are not concerned to defend a naturalistic worldview, they fail to point out that its advocates can find and adopt meaning by an act of faith not unlike the one necessary for a Christian worldview.

The penultimate chapter analyzes Carl Sagan's public television series, "Cosmos." The authors praise its "vividly illustrated presentation of the contemporary, scientifically derived picture of the physical universe." But, they say, "What Sagan failed to point out is that, although natural science chooses to limit the object of its investigation to the physical universe, that does not provide any warrant for asserting that 'the Cosmos is all there is or ever was or ever will be'." They conclude that, "By failing to honor the boundaries of the scientific domain, by transforming natural science into naturalistic scientism and by presenting science as the victor over theism, 'Cosmos' misrepresented the character of the scientific enterprise... [It] was religious theater — an evangelistic crusade for modern Western naturalism."

In their Epilogue, the authors introduce the term "folk science" to label what occurs "when the epistemic goal of gaining knowledge is replaced by the dogmatic goal of providing warrant for one's personal belief system or for some sectarian creed... Those of us who are educators ought to recognize folk science as serving a function very different from that of professional natural science."

My worldview differs substantially from that of the authors: I am agnostic regarding the nature of ultimate reality (though not regarding ethics). But those of us who are educators on the public payroll are not paid to promote our own religion or worldview. We are paid to help students see how specific assumptions and evidence are — or are not — connected to specific conclusions. Contrary to the claims of "creation scientists," science, including those parts of it that deal with evolutionary concepts, is not a religion or worldview. This is because its naturalism is methodological, not ontological. It may be that the education of professional educators at all levels should include more emphasis on making the kinds of distinctions that *Science Held Hostage* effectively advocates.

Karl D. Fezer
Department of Biology
Concord College
Athens, WV 24712

THE GENESIS FLOOD
The Biblical Record and Its Scientific Implications

by John C. Whitcomb, Jr. and Henry M. Morris
Presbyterian and Reformed Publishing Company
Philadelphia, PA (1961, 23rd printing 1979)

The Genesis Flood presents a clear basis for evaluating much of the current interest in "scientific creationism." The publication of *The Genesis Flood* over three decades ago stirred up a great deal of interest in a group of Christian apologeticists seeking to unite Biblical literalism with evidence from the geological and biological sciences. In this historical context, the publication of *The Genesis Flood* was one of the catalysts that helped foster the current creationist movement. Both authors have remained prominent figures in the movement. Morris, who has a Ph.D. in engineering from the University of Minnesota, now serves as Director of the San Diego-based Institute for Creation Research. Whitcomb is a Th.D. from Grace Theological Seminary. In this volume the two have combined their efforts to present a series of scriptural exegeses and scientific conjectures and assertions that focus on the Biblical story of Noah, and the global flood described therein.

The book catalog of the Institute of Creation Research described *The Genesis Flood* as "the most comprehensive scientific exposition of creation and the flood, providing the best system for unifying and correlating scientific data bearing on the earth's early history." Although this description suggests that the volume is primarily scientific in scope, much of the text is devoted to scriptural and theological arguments. The authors devoted the greatest portion of text to an exposition of geological ideas that purportedly demonstrate two general themes: 1) most of the earth's sedimentary rock record and its contained fossils were deposited during a single global hydraulic cataclysm several thousand years ago, and 2) virtually all of the major conclusions of the geological sciences are seriously in error. In particular, they suggest that uniformitarian ideas cannot adequately explain the bulk of the geologic record.

Specific geologic examples and quotes are so numerous in *The Genesis Flood* that a point-by-point rebuttal of the inaccuracies and logical flaws in Whitcomb and Morris' arguments would require hundreds of pages. Therein lies the strength of their book — the "evidence" they present appears overwhelming, and cannot be adequately evaluated by people unfamiliar with geologic methods. However, the reader should remember that no original geologic research was undertaken by either author — all of their "evidence" was borrowed from the work of others, primarily geologists who disagree with virtually all of their conclusions. Whitcomb and Morris suggest that the geological sciences have been blinded by an inflexible dogma of uniformitarianism, and, therefore, geologists have failed to recognize evidence for the great hydraulic cataclysm of Noah's day.

Yet such an analysis is primarily based on a grossly inaccurate presentation of uniformitarian principles used in geology. For example, they claimed that "to be consistent with uniformitarianism the various types of sedimentary rocks must all be interpreted in terms of so-called environments of deposition exactly equivalent to present-day situations." Yet more correctly, uniformitarianism postulates that the same basic processes operate throughout geological history, not that the environments, situations, consequences, and results are necessarily identical at different times. Gross inaccuracies of this sort pervade the volume. The scientific "evidence" presented in the volume is essentially a series of speculations with little or no factual scientific basis. Where evidence is supplied, it is generally in the form of highly selective quotes from the geological literature.

Although the scientific merits of the volume are limited, the authors of *The Genesis Flood* deserve credit for clearly presenting the real basis for their creationist interpretations. Many of the more recent books on "scientific creationism" attempt to cloak the real basis for creationist ideas by presenting the Genesis story in scientific jargon without scriptural reference. Whitcomb and Morris openly admit that their interpretations are "founded squarely on full confidence in the Scriptures." With this basis they suggest that "the false presuppositions and implications of organic evolution and geologic uniformitarianism need to be challenged in the name of Holy Scripture." Although the authors attempt to use geologic information to strengthen their story, they admit that

> ... the real issue is not the correctness of the interpretation of various details of the geologic data, but simply what God has revealed in His Word concerning these matters. This is why the first four chapters and the two appendixes are devoted to a detailed exposition and analysis of the Biblical teachings on creation, the Flood, and related topics.

However, in science the issue *is* the analysis of the details of the geologic data, not the details of scriptural interpretation. Hence, *The Genesis Flood* is primarily a theological, not a scientific, discourse. The authors' rejection of the major conclusions of the geological sciences is not based on the strength of their scientific arguments, but on their own scriptural framework. Their religious beliefs interface with science when they attempt to

> ... build a true science of earth history on the framework revealed in the Bible, rather than on uniformitarian and evolutionary assumptions ... letting the Bible speak for itself and then trying to understand the geological data in light of its teachings.

This approach is the antithesis of the scientific method — it is based on the authority of religious dogma and not on multiple working hypotheses. The primary intent of Whitcomb and Morris when they wrote *The Genesis Flood* was apparently evangelical, as reflected by a quote from the preface to the sixth printing:

> It is our sincere prayer that God may continue to use this volume for the purpose of restoring His people everywhere to full reliance on the truth of the Biblical doctrine of origins.

In conclusion, I can recommend *The Genesis Flood* to those interested in the historical development of ideas in the creationist movement. The volume still stands as the lengthiest creationist assault on conventional geological ideas yet published. However, for three reasons I cannot recommend its use in public school science classes: 1) it contains numerous scientific inaccuracies, 2) scientific methods are not utilized and scriptural interpretations remain preeminent, and 3) numerous scriptural exegeses and evangelical overtones are clearly sectarian and outside the realm of science.

Brian J. Witzke
Research Geologist
Iowa Department of Natural Resources
Geological Survey Bureau, and
Adjunct Assistant Professor
Department of Geology
University of Iowa
Iowa City, IA 52242

THE NATURAL SCIENCES KNOW NOTHING OF EVOLUTION

by A.E. Wilder-Smith
Creation-Life Publishers
San Diego, CA (1977)

This book is one of a long line of works by English authors who consciously strive to be wildly iconoclastic. As with many of these efforts, it ends up not as iconoclasm but as a mixture of arrogance and scientific ignorance.

The title would suggest that the book deals with evolution; however, only one chapter does in fact do so. Most of the book (five of seven chapters) is devoted to the question of spontaneous development of life on earth. While this field of study is related to evolution, they are hardly the same. Most basic knowledge of evolution predates any scientific study of biogenesis, and would be unaffected by any theory concerning the origin of life.

One additional chapter (Chapter Six) is devoted to a critique of certain dating methods, and only Chapter Seven and part of Chapter One and the appendix deal with evolution. Throughout, the author displays a consistent misunderstanding of the topics under consideration. At the start of his discussion he defines science as "... experimental science; that is, ... those sciences which deal with definite, experimental, regularly repeatable results ..." (p. 1), thus eliminating not only evolution but astronomy, geography, and many other sciences. Having started with this fundamental misunderstanding of science, his conclusions are hardly surprising.

The most fundamental flaw of the book is an apparent confusion or ignorance (it is hard to tell which) concerning our present understanding of the evolutionary process. The theoretical aspect of evolution is discussed to some extent, but the factual aspect of evolution – the sequential change in organism types – is never dealt with. The latter is simply ignored; yet this is the primary basis of scientific understanding and acceptance of the validity of the evolutionary process. The only nod given to 250 years of accumulated paleontological-phylogenetic evolutionary data is a five-and-a-half page diatribe against index fossils. It is as though someone writing a 164 page book on medicine should spend most of the book talking about hospital administration and deal with disease for only five-and-a-half pages, devoting this largely to criticism about the methods of using antibiotics.

The second major flaw in the book is a woeful disregard of the basic phenomena and literature in the field discussed. For example, in Wilder-Smith's prolix discussion of the problem of chirality (optical activity by biological molecules), many of the most significant contributions in this field are not cited, while one of Eigen's early studies is discussed at length. The author's apparent ignorance concerning theories of the origin of life is also displayed in his extended attempt to show (p. 14) that oceans, as they presently exist, could not be the place where life originated. Yet, few if any modern students of biogenesis even consider this possibility. The most fundamental flaw is his heavy emphasis on the impossibility of biogenesis without logos or rules. What he seems not to comprehend is that there has never been any question of the presence of a logos. The only question is where it is encoded. Students of the chemical origin of life feel that it is encoded in the chemicals which made up the primitive earth. Wilder-Smith apparently feels it is encoded elsewhere, although "where" never becomes clear. He also is seemingly unaware that most of the planning of biogenesis experiments is done to mimic conditions which would have occurred on the primitive earth, and can thus hardly represent a plan in his sense of a present organization.

In his discussion of the second law of thermodynamics it is indeed a revelation to learn that "... the behavior of matter in a thermodynamically open system does not differ much, at least from the standpoint of auto-organization, from that of a closed system...." Such a statement denies the possibility of the growth of a tree or the formation of a galaxy, as well as the spontaneous chemical origin of life.

His critique of dating techniques reveals a serious lack of information. First, in his long discussion of ^{14}C dating he ignores the fact that the most recent improvements of the method have produced results only slightly discrepant with those of dendrochonology. He is oblivious to the many other dating methods such as varve analysis, paleomagnetism, etc., and to the fact that all these methods produce data in close agreement with each other and with radiometric methods.

All of these shortcomings shrink into insignificance when, however, the reader becomes aware of Wilder-Smith's astounding lack of knowledge of evolution and biology. First, he is apparently unaware of the host of data from comparative anatomy, embryology, biochemistry and physiology supporting the occurrence of evolution. Second, he is apparently unaware of the distinction between phyletic extinction and species extinction and consistently treats them as one and the same. Third, he seems to subscribe to the long outdated view that evolution is necessarily progressive and "upward moving." No serious student of evolution any longer supports this view. Throughout the book his ignorance of basic biology is impressive. Perhaps the best example of this is his statement that, "We know of no intermediate stages between invertebrate octopus and squid types and genuine vertebrates" (p. 131). One could equally well say we know of no intermediates between oak trees and man, but his hardly bears on evolutionary concepts.

In summary, this book, while it is occasionally amusing, is science-trash. It does not belong in a science classroom.

Kenneth Christiansen
Professor of Biology
Grinnell College
Grinnell, IA 50112

THE CREATION-EVOLUTION CONTROVERSY

by R.L. Wysong, D.V.M.
Inquiry Press
Midland, MI (1975)

At first glance this work creates the hope of seeing a balanced treatment of the controversy cited; however, a close reading dashes this hope. Evolutionary science is equated with complete amorality as is shown in the following conversation (p.3):

> To illustrate the relationship between origins and life-philosophy, a student asks a learned group gathered for a discussion: "Why does man seem to be continually at war?"
>
> "That's the nature of man," someone answers.
>
> "Why?" the student retorts.
>
> Another in the group follows up, "War is simply a part of social evolution. Why we even see the violent struggles for survival among the animals. War is the means by which the earth's population is kept in check and the weak societies are culled to make room for the more fit. So, you see, war actually serves for the betterment of the human race in the long run."
>
> Feeling a cold chill the student replies, "Isn't that inhuman? Isn't it wrong to kill others? I certainly don't want to be one of those sacrificed for the 'betterment of the human race'."
>
> "Who is to say what is right or wrong? Our primary responsibility is to ourselves and what we feel is right for the occasion," pops back another in the group.

Neither the source of these quotations nor the identity of the "learned group" is given. A little later evolution is equated with both Nazism and Communism. It is clear that what we are about to read will hardly be a dispassionate analysis of the issue. We are not to be disappointed in this expectation. For example, in dealing with the use of expert testimony, Wysong says (p. 19):

> Evolutionists agree to the historicity, actuality, reality, and fact of evolution. There is, however, no consensus on the exact mechanism by which the process took place. Thus we will find evolutionary expert vying with evolutionary expert on all facets of the proposed evolutionary scheme.

He then proceeds to discuss in some detail the areas of disagreement, but never again mentions the agreement or the reasons for such agreement. This can hardly be considered balanced treatment. This work is not really a treatment of the controversy between creationism and evolution, but rather a long defense of creationist views decked out as a balanced treatment. Wysong achieves his result by organizing a series of false confrontations and by using a large number of references from scientific literature.

The first technique is shown, for example, when he attempts to discredit evolution by subtly misdefining key concepts (p.43):

> If the materialist's proposition is a scientific hypothesis, then it must be based upon observed phenomena — according to definition. Are scientists observing the spontaneous generation of life today in test tubes, swamps, or mud puddles? Or are organisms observed evolving into new and different organisms? No, they are not! If that be the case, and evolution is still considered a scientific hypothesis, then a trained scientist must have observed and recorded the original formation of life. Likewise, scientists must have observed evolution through the hundreds of millions of years it is said to have taken place.

He here concentrates on the origin of life, ignoring the fact that while this question is an outgrowth of evolutionary thought, it has nothing directly to do either with the factual occurrence of evolution or with explanations of its mechanism. (Wysong also ignores the fact that biological chemists are doing test-tube studies of many aspects of the origin of life.) He sets up a second false confrontation by asserting that a scientific hypothesis can only deal with directly observed phenomena. This view eliminates from science most of modern physics and chemistry; no one has yet observed electrons moving in orbit.

The second technique, the extensive use of quotations, is at first impressive; but when one examines the works quoted, one finds that they are either: (a) from creationist sources, or (b) taken out of context and twisted to fit the author's presuppositions. For example, C.A. Reed is quoted to show the invalidity of ^{14}C dating:

> C.A. Reed writes similarly regarding the ^{14}C method:
>
> > Although it was hailed as the answer to the prehistorian's prayer when it was first announced, there has been increasing disillusion with the method because of the chronological uncertainties, in some cases absurdities, that would follow a strict adherence to ^{14}C dates ... What bids to become a classic example of "^{14}C irresponsibility" is the 6000 year spread of eleven determinations for Jarmo, a prehistoric village in northeastern Iraq, which, on the basis of archaeological evidence, was not occupied for more than 500 consecutive years.

Below I reprint the deleted section represented by the ellipsis in Wysong's above quotation:

> This is not a question of the physical laws underlying the principle used, or the accuracy of the counters now in operation around the world; the unsolved problem, instead, seems to lie in the difficulty of securing samples completely free from either older or younger adherent carbon. At least to the present, no kind or degree of chemical cleaning can guarantee one-age carbon, typical only of the time of the site from which it was excavated. (1)

A second argument against the validity of ^{14}C dating involves Wysong's very selective summary of a 1963 article by Keith and Anderson (2): "Living mollusks (snails, etc.) have had their shells (misdated) by the ^{14}C method up to 2,300 years."

Following is the authors' summary of this article:

Abstract. Evidence is presented to show that modern mollusk shells from rivers can have anomalous radiocarbon ages, owing mainly to incorporation of inactive (carbon-14 deficient) carbon from humus, probably through the food web, as well as by the pathway of carbon dioxide from humus decay. The resultant effect, in addition to the variable contributions of atmospheric carbon dioxide, fermentative carbon dioxide from bottom muds, and, locally, of carbonate carbon from dissolving limestones, makes the initial carbon-14 activity of ancient fresh-water shells indeterminate, but within limits. Consequent errors of shell radiocarbon dates may be as large as several thousand years for river shells.

The authors here point out a special circumstance — the recycling of older biological carbon — which makes ^{14}C dating inapplicable to riverine mollusk shells. Such self correction and identification of sources of error give validity to scientific results. Wysong improperly uses correction of error to invalidate the dating method. Such distortion is general throughout the work.

Some of the problems with the book may stem from simple ignorance. For example, when in Chapter Three he attempts to establish the existence of only two views of the origin of life — the creationist model and the scientific evolutionist model — his failure to note the cyclic religious evolutionist views of the Hindu and Buddhist religions may result from ignorance. Similarly, when he states (p. 164) that dendrochronology has produced no ages older than 5,000 years, or when he ignores such independent dating mechanisms as varve counting or obsidian aging, there errors may also be due to ignorance. It is almost certainly ignorance which leads him to conclude erroneously (p. 327) that plants which botanists consider advanced should be more flourishing than those which display "primitive" [sic] features. But it is more difficult to accept the ideas that he really thinks that "we are also faced with the clear evidence that about two-thirds of the earth's geological record, the 'Pre-Cambrian period,' does not contain any significant quantities of indisputable fossils (some contend it contains absolutely none)," (p. 362) when we have large numbers of such fossils. It is also difficult to accept the idea that he is unaware of the fraudulent nature of the Paluxy "human footprint" fossils that he illustrates (p. 367).

In summary, this work gives the superficial appearance of being a balanced treatment of the controversy concerning creationism; however, a close reading shows that it is in fact a religious tract aimed at presenting largely distorted or spurious arguments to support a single recent creation. Its biased and misleading nature render the book wholly unsuitable for use in teaching legitimate science.

References

1. C.A. Reed 1959. "Animal domestication in the prehistoric Near East." **Science** 130:1630.
2. M. Keith and G. Anderson 1963. "Radiocarbon dating: Fictitious results with mollusk shells." **Science** 141:634.

Kenneth Christiansen
Professor of Biology
Grinnell College
Grinnell, IA 50112

CHRISTIANITY AND THE AGE OF THE EARTH

by Davis A. Young
Zondervan Publishing House
Grand Rapids MI (1982)
(Currently available from
Artisan Sales, P.O. Box 1497, Thousand Oaks CA 91360)

SCIENCE, SCRIPTURE, AND THE YOUNG EARTH
An Answer to Current Arguments against the Biblical Doctrine of Recent Creation

by Henry M. Morris
Institute for Creation Research
El Cajon CA (1983)

If oak trees and humans share a common ancestor, that ancestor had to live very long ago. Henry Morris' literal interpretation of Genesis convinces him that God created the universe less than 10,000 years ago, that he created each "kind" of organism separately, and that he triggered and managed a Flood that lasted a year and covered the entire earth. The evidence in nature, "rightly interpreted," must point to the same conclusions. And if by scientific reasoning the earth can be shown to be young, what a fine way to discredit evolution! This has been a significant part of the program of "scientific" creationism, a movement of which Morris is the acknowledged pioneer and leader.

Davis Young, Professor of Geology at Calvin College, shares Morris' belief in Biblical inerrancy but insists that there are many possible interpretations of God's inerrant word, all of which seem to present some difficulties. Therefore the conclusions of science, which is a separate and distinct way of understanding the universe, should also be considered seriously. Young sees Biblical exegesis and scientific reasoning as separate enterprises, each with its own assumptions and rules, each fallible, and he insists that they not be confused. If they lead to contradictory conclusions, well, these "are not real conflicts between nature and the Bible, but only conflicts between natural science and theological exegesis."

Without elaborating, Young opposes "a materialist evolutionary philosophy" and the "doctrine of the evolution of man," apparently on religious grounds. But in the scientific part of his book, as its title indicates, Young is concerned only to show why "scientific evidence considered as a whole, and as we have it now, compellingly argues for the great antiquity of the Earth." The book as a whole is devoted to showing why "scientific" creationism is bad science (and bad theology). Young shows that it is "based on incomplete information, wishful thinking, ignorance of real geological situations, selective use of data to support the favored hypothesis, and faulty reasoning." His apparent motive: "'Proving' the Bible or Christianity with a spurious scientific hypothesis can only be injurious to the cause of Christ."

Part One of Young's book (55 pages) usefully traces concepts regarding the age of the earth in church history, as influenced more and more in the last few centuries by the developing science of geology. Part Two (61 pages) contains chapters dealing with various kinds of sedimentary deposits, radiometric dating, the earth's magnetic field, and geochemical arguments. For each topic Young reviews creationist arguments and shows why they collapse. Some of this narrative, for example the chapter on radiometric dating, constitutes a good primer on the topics discussed. Part Three (30 pages) discusses "philosophical and apologetic considerations." One chapter discusses creationist misuse of the concepts of uniformitarianism and catastrophism, and the final chapter offers principles, alluded to above, as to how believers in Biblical inerrancy can seek to reconcile their faith and science without doing violence to either one.

Among the faithful, Young's book constitutes more of a challenge to "scientific" creationism than a dozen books by nonbelievers, and Morris wasted no time in issuing his response. *Science, Scripture, and the Young Earth*, a 34-page pamphlet, explicitly aims to discredit Young and his "more important" arguments. Morris is a skillful polemicist; as usual, his arguments are superficially persuasive, especially because he quotes noncreationist scientists in a way that seems to support his arguments. But even readers who, like this reviewer, are not geologists can detect plenty of evidence to support Young's charges of poor (shifty?) scholarship. For example, in describing rubidium-strontium dating by the whole-rock isochron method, Young says that it is most reliable for dating igneous rocks. In challenging a basic assumption of this method, Morris cites papers by his own disciples, none published in refereed journals. Morris also quotes passages from four more reputable sources which seem, at first glance, to support his arguments. But one quotation actually implies that the problem Morris cites is not serious for older rocks — that is, for dates that most effectively refute Morris' young-earth hypothesis. All of the three other quotations refer to rocks that are sedimentary or metamorphic, not igneous, a fact easily missed by the casual reader.

The "scientific" argument for a young earth that Morris cites most frequently in his writings and speeches is based on the earth's decaying magnetic field and was developed by his colleague Thomas G. Barnes. Young explains why it is in scientific disrepute. Morris' response is, in part, a testimonial for Barnes. But Barnes' argument has also been debunked by Stephen G. Brush (*Journal of Geological Education* 30:53, 1982; also see Brush's review in this volume). To illustrate the obsolescence of Barnes' argument, Brush noted that, in an article published in 1981, Barnes quoted as his clinching evidence a passage from a book by J. A. Jacobs in which evidence for reversals of the earth's magnetic field was questioned. Barnes failed to mention that Jacobs' book was published in 1963 and that, in the 1975 edition, Jacobs reversed his assessment. In 1983 Barnes published a revised edition of his *Origin and Destiny of the Earth's Magnetic Field*, allegedly with a response to Brush's criticisms. In fact, most of Brush's criticisms are ignored. Indeed, Barnes' 1983 version culminates with the same quotation from Jacobs' 1963 edition, and again there is no reference to the date of this quotation or to the 1975 revision.

Morris does neatly pinpoint the difference between his approach and Young's: "Young makes it plain that his real reasons for holding the long-age view are geological rather than Biblical. In so doing, he renders those of us who believe the Biblical record is inerrant, authoritative, and perspicuous a real service. The data of geology, in our view, should be interpreted in light of Scripture, rather than distorting Scripture to accommodate current geological philosophy." Both men agree that the Bible is inerrant, but Morris, in claiming that it is also perspicuous, in effect denies that it, like nature, must be interpreted — a view that he cannot consistently sustain. And in establishing his interpretation of Scripture as a decisive consideration in scientific reasoning he renders his own reasoning unscientific.

Those many Christians who do not regard the Bible as inerrant may be baffled by both Morris and Young. But Young clearly distinguishes between scientific reasoning, in which resort to miracles has no place, and his own evangelical religious commitments. A system of thought should be defined in terms of whatever consensus on assumptions and rules exists among those who recognize one another as practitioners of the system. The worldviews of scientists vary widely. The consensus among them is of more limited scope. Therefore science should not be thought of as a worldview. A person's religious beliefs do not exclude him or her from the scientific community so long as these beliefs are not allowed to distort the practice of science.

Young, a believing creationist, accepts the geological evidence for an old earth. He says, "The totality of the evidence just does not point to the Earth being only a few thousand years old, no matter how ardently creationists might wish that it did. No amount of juggling can change the overwhelming weight of the evidence." At the same time, Young apparently does not find the weight of evidence for evolution, and especially for human evolution, equally compelling. He seems to admit the influence of his doctrinal position on this judgment. One wonders whether his standards for evaluation of biological evidence are the same as for his own field of geology.

Nevertheless, one must respect Young's work. If one wishes to give students a book that is candid and scholarly and yet written by an author committed to the principle of biblical inerrancy, this could be the book. Young, and others who share his views, can contribute significantly to educating the public, and especially their fellow evangelicals, on the nature of that limited enterprise called science. Morris, on the other hand, clearly does let his religious views distort his attempts to reason scientifically. His enterprise is quite different from science. Much of the creation/evolution controversy would vanish if he and his fellow "scientific" creationists frankly acknowledged this; such a step, however, is tactically impossible for them.

Addendum: In 1989 the Institute for Creation Research published an "enlarged [to 95 pages] and updated" edition of *Science, Scripture, and the Young Earth*, with Henry's son, John D. Morris, added as junior author. The authors note the "anti-creationist reaction of many Christian evangelical intellectuals," but identify the writings of Davis Young, and especially the book reviewed above, as "probably the most influential." Therefore the new edition continues to focus on Young's arguments. The authors also refer to the more recent *Science Held Hostage*, of which Young is co-author (see review, p. 128 this volume), as an "anti-creationist diatribe," but they fail to respond to its charge that "creation-scientists" routinely ignore relevant evidence.

In 1984 I wrote a detailed, line-by-line analysis and critique of a one-and-a-half page section of the first edition of Morris' pamphlet, documenting extensive misrepresentation of the sources he quoted. I sent him the manuscript for comment. Included in Morris' reply were objections to two specific points, which I then modified in the published version of my article ("Dr. Morris and the Green River Formation." *Creation/Evolution Newsletter* 5(6):16-20, November/December 1985). So Morris evidently did read my critique. Yet the discussion of the Green River Formation in the new edition of his booklet is almost identical to that in the earlier edition, with a few points added at the end.

The new edition includes a ten-page appendix, "Recent ICR Research on the Age of the Earth." This, we are told, includes a study of carbon-14 dating methods. Because of the short half-life of that isotope, scientists regard this method as irrelevant to determining the age of the earth. But at ICR, "our desire is to salvage the C-14 method ... for of all radioactive decay methods, this is the only one which addresses the last few thousand years." The authors "feel" that certain unidentified "discrepancies" are "due to the flood — a time during which the pre-flood carbon inventory was drastically changed, in part due to the precipitation of vast amounts of limestone." Other ICR "research" is devoted to interpreting the Grand Canyon, Mt. Saint Helens, other rock formations, the helium content of the atmosphere, and the sodium content of the oceans as evidence for a young earth.

Davis Young, in a telephone interview in July 1992, said he was puzzled as to why Zondervan declared his book out-of-print fairly soon after publishing it, even though it had gone through four printings and was still selling briskly. Zondervan is an evangelical publishing house. Someone like me, predisposed to be suspicious, might suspect that young-earth creationists persuaded Zondervan's management to drop Young's book. The book is again available — reproduced from a photocopy of Zondervan's fourth printing (which incorporated some minor revisions).

Karl D, Fezer
Professor of Biology
Concord College
Athens, WV 24712

APPENDIX

Books on the Creation/Evolution Controversy

Niles Eldredge, 1982. **The Monkey Business: A Scientist Looks at Creationism**. New York: Washington Square Press (Pocket Books).

Raymond A. Eve & Francis B. Harold, 1991. **The Creationist Movement in Modern America**. Boston: Twayne Publishers, G.K. Hall & Company.

Douglas J. Futuyma, 1983. **Science on Trial: The Case for Evolution**. New York: Pantheon.

Laurie Godfrey, 1988. **Scientists Confront Creationism**. New York: W.W. Norton.

Philip Kitcher, 1982. **Abusing Science: The Case Against Creationism**. Cambridge: MIT Press.

Edward J. Larson, 1989. **Trial and Error: The American Controversy over Creation and Evolution**. New York: Oxford University Press.

Betty McCollister, 1989. **Voices for Evolution**. Berkeley, CA: The National Center for Science Education, Inc.

Tom McIver, 1988. **Anti-Evolution: An Annotated Bibliography**. Jefferson, NC: McFarland.

Ashley Montagu, 1984. **Science and Creationism**. New York: Oxford University Press.

Norman D. Newell, 1982. **Creation or Evolution: Myth or Reality?** New York: Columbia University Press.

Michael Ruse, 1988. **But Is It Science? The Philosophical Question in the Creation/Evolution Controversy**. Buffalo, NY: Prometheus Press.

Arthur Strahler, 1989. **Science and Earth History: The Evolution/Creation Controversy**. Buffalo, NY: Prometheus Press.

Index — Book Titles Reviewed

Index — Reviewers